Around Dane Valley

Gradbach to Bosley

Haymaking at Gradbach Old Hall. Downes family and neighbours c.1950.

Compiled by Sheila Hine

Front Cover: John and Mary Nadin
Back Cover: Top, Freda and Anson at Higher Minn End, Bosley
Bottom, Wincle

CHURNET VALLEY BOOKS
1 King Street, Leek, Staffordshire. ST13 5NW 01538 399033 www.leekbooks.co.uk
© Sheila Hine and Churnet Valley Books 2014
ISBN 9781904546993

CONTENTS

ACKNOWLEDGEMENTS

Thanks to all the people who have contributed stories and photographs.
And to Margaret Mullins for proof-reading.

Thank you: To Cynthia Edwards for the information and photos she has gathered about the Bosley area and to the Swythamley Historical Society and Geoff and Jean Fisher for the use of some photos.

This book has been produced as part of the Dane Valley Woodland Project with support from the Heritage Lottery Fund through the Peak District National Park Authority

Supported by
The National Lottery®
through the Heritage Lottery Fund

heritage
lottery fund

Danebridge Mill c.1918

Introduction

The valley and tributaries of the River Dane from its source on the Axe Edge moors to Bosley is still largely unspoiled and very beautiful; some parts like the valley of the Shell Brook feel remote and romantic. The upper areas have some moorland and the farms are upland with steep valley sides which are often wooded. This wooded character is what makes the area almost unique within the Peak District. It is an area crossed with old packhorse tracks and full of tales and legends. In the past there would have been the scars of industry which are now grown over and softened by nature.

Not far from the source of the river were the Reeve Edge and Dane Bower quarries and moving down the river valley coal was mined both from shafts and bell pits. The area would have been populated with people living within walking distance of these and other industries. By Manor Farm at Gradbach were beds where ochre was settled out from the brook and then sold on as pigment for paints.

There were several mills on the river: Gradbach Mill and Folly Mill, then further down Danebridge Mill and Wincle or Whitelee Mill, which were both associated with James Brindley. Nearby was Bearda Mill and further downstream Bosley Mills, also associated with Brindley.

There was a forge recorded at Gradbach in the 1700s which would have been driven by a waterwheel. This is thought to have been where the car park is now on the way to Gradbach Mill. Further along is Castors Bridge where smelting may have taken place. (*Walk Past Gradbach*. Margaret Parker 2006)

Legend has it that here was a cottage where travellers would be taken in by an old lady and her daughter. They would be murdered for their goods and money and their bodies disposed of in the stove. Further along there is the natural chasm of Ludchurch with its stories of the Lollards. The legend of Sir Gawain and the Green Knight is also linked to here and to Castors Bridge.

Danebridge is first mentioned in 1357; the old way crossed the river by Slider Ford, so called because the shaly banks were so slippery. (*Peakland Roads and Trackways*. AE & EM Dodd 2000) The road is thought to have continued past Wincle Grange which was built by the monks of Combermere Abbey in the 14thC and still has ecclesiastical windows in the gable end.

The Swythamley and Danebridge area is more lately famed for the Brocklehurst's Estate and the tree-lined lanes are a legacy of their planting. They were particularly fond of trees and tenants were very rarely allowed to take timber. However in the past the woodlands were the

Wincle Grange

scene of much more intensive management than in recent years with evidence of coppicing and clear felling to produce wood products for local and regional use. It is known that timber was taken from Barleyford Wood to the copper mines at Ecton in the late 18thC (*The Dukes Manor*. Lindsey Porter 2012) and it is also likely that they played a role in providing timber for the Napoleonic war effort. In spring the woodlands are particularly beautiful with swathes of bluebells and the fresh green of new leaves. In the earlier part of the last century a very popular walking excursion was from Rushton along the Feeder path and continuing by the river to Danebridge. Many visitors came to Rushton by train to walk here.

From Hug Bridge the valley opens out into a more pastoral scene towards the Bosley Mills with richer farmland. Bosley was an important area being on the main Derby to Manchester road and having the railway and the canal. There are secret valleys like Swallowdale with tributaries feeding Bosley Reservoir and the Dane.

We finish our journey on the hills overlooking Bosley with remnants of heather moor. On Bosley Minn there are views back up the Dane Valley to Quarnford and the other way over the Cheshire Plain where the Dane winds its way along until it joins the River Weaver.

There is much old history well documented in many places but this is a more personal account with memories mainly from the last century to give a flavour of life in the area in a time which doesn't seem so long ago but has already seen so many changes.

Further reading:
The South-West Peak, History of The Landscape. Eric Wood 2000
Dane Mills Bosley. Chris R Pownall 2012.
Bosley. A brief history from William the Conqueror to 1939, Rev JWA Greenacre. (Bosley Church.)

Folly Mill

Philip Hooley

Parks Farm 1951

My grandparents, George and Annie Kirkham rented this farm called Parks at Gradbach from Lord Derby. My mum, Florence worked at the Crag Inn for the Sharpleys where she was a maid and barmaid, looked after the pub and lived in there. It was wartime and there were Dutch soldiers billeted in Wildboarclough. My father, James Hooley, was born and lived at Helmesley where he worked for his brother Frank. The farm was also rented from Lord Derby. In 1945 my parents married and moved in here and my grandparents moved up to Top Parks.

Originally my Granny Hooley had farmed Helmesley; she lost her husband when he was 49 but bought up three children, my father, Uncle Frank and Aunty Evelyn. She farmed 100 acres and kept about 20 cows and 60 sheep and also had a workman and a maid; a remarkable woman.

At Top Parks they kept pigs and hens and Grandad had a job as lengthsman for the council. He was responsible for the road from the Rose and Crown at Allgreave up to the Cat and Fiddle and walked over the tops to do that five days in the week.

Philip

In 1953 the outlying farms of the estate were sold; Bennetsitch, Parks, Knar and Cut-thorn could all together have been bought for under £8000. This farm was 216 acres, Bennetsitch 105, and Knar and Cut-thorn both similar. Dad bought this farm, Grandad bought Top Parks and Uncle Frank bought Helmesley.

I went to school at Wildboarclough; my brother Alan and I walked down and caught the taxi at Dane Cottage where Mrs Dodd used to take us in to wait. If we missed it Mother used to make us walk over the tops and down Hall Lane to school. We used to go up through Top Parks yard and granny would say, 'Why don't you stop here? but we didn't dare. We landed at school about 10 o'clock.

I spent a lot of time at Top Parks. They kept pigs in the building on the end of the house and in one across the yard and there were hencotes dotted all round the fields. They had to carry water from a tank to all the hens and pigs; my granny used to have a yoke and buckets. There was no water in the cottage either; it was buckets all day and in winter everything frozen up.

DANE COTTAGE.

When I was ten I used to go mole catching for Wilf Massey at Berry Bank, Stephen Slack at Knar, Charlie Brown at Birchenbooth and Dicky Rider who had Gradbach Mill then. I used to go at weekends, on foot with about 6 traps and get sixpence for each mole caught. The traps had been in the ground all week and I might have caught 3 moles but it was a lot of money then.

Dad had a horse called Bess and these meadows below, about 15 acres, he mowed with a horse mower and we used to work it by hand as kids; turning it, tedding and putting it into footcocks. The weather seemed to be atrocious; we had hay down a month and worked it time and time again, moving it all the time and then fetching it up from the bottom. I can see it now, Bess with the cart with thrippers on front and back and poles on the corners and loose hay on bouncing along. We had some good crops but it was the weather we didn't have - there were some terrible summers. Later on a chap called Bert Heathcote from Black Clough above Knotbury started mowing with a Standard Fordson; he cut the iron wheels off the mower and put rubber ones on so he could go on the road with it. He came to mow for us and later had a baler as well; we thought that was marvellous but the trouble was getting him - everyone wanted him. Bess lived to a good age; dad had to have her put down in the end.

We milked about 30 cows here and when I left school in 1963 we built up to 45. We finished milking in 1975. At that time I also reared 1200 calves a year up to 15 weeks old on contract. We had about 200 sheep; later when I had bought Cut-thorn land I would be lambing 1000 ewes. The milking was all by hand; we had no electric until the mid-50s so had to use lanterns and Tilley lamps. The electric was put on in the winter in terrible weather; I remember coming back from school and we could see a TV ariel on the roof - we were that excited.

I remember one day when Bryan Worsley worked for us, all the roads were full of

Bryan Worsley with Philip and Joyce Whittaker

Joyce, Philip and Bryan with Bess, and Glen the dog

Bryan and Mrs Kirkham at Top Parks in 1947

snow so Bryan and dad went with Bess and a wooden sledge with four churns of milk tied onto it and they went all the way to the Ryles Arms at Sutton which was as far as the wagon could get and a man from the Co-op had left bread there for us. They left here about 10 in the morning and I think it was about 4 in the afternoon when they got back; it must be at least 6 miles.

I went to school in Macclesfield when I was eleven and when we were lambing - we had Gritstones then - dad went milking and I used to get up about 6am and walk round all the tops and then the bottom to look all the sheep, then tell dad what was happening before getting ready and being down the bottom to catch the school bus for 8 o'clock.

We kept hens on the loft above the shippons and mother used to keep pigs; she had in the teens of sows and all the young ones. We lost them all with Swine Fever in 1963 just before I left school. Mother had taken two gilts down to Mr Parks farm near to the Ryles Arms to the boar and it must have come from there and it started in our little pigs. There was a lot of snow and ice packed hard against the doors, halfway up; we had to dig down to get into the buildings, the snow and ice kept building up. I wanted to stay at home but they made me go to school. They came and shot all the pigs, dragged them out and took them away then power washed everything. My mother cried her eyes out - she was heart broken.

There were two air crashes nearby; in January 1945 a B17 Flying Fortress bomber crashed on Birchenough Hill above here. It was dark and dad and Uncle Frank were milking at Helmesley. They heard this plane coming very low and then the thud of the crash. They left the milking and ran up Helmesley Hill thinking it was just over that hill but no, then over Goosetree farm but not there, onto Parks Farm..... and by the time they got to it Dutch soldiers from out of Wildboarclough were up there guarding it. A lot of the common was on fire and five men were killed.

A few years later our neighbour Bob Lane from Bennetsitch was fetching his horses in. It was foggy when two Seafire planes came past him literally only yards away. The horses bolted and the planes crashed through the wall and onto Tagsclough Hill where both pilots were killed. It was thought that they had collided in mid air.

We used to have a lot of peewits; you don't see many now, they can't survive the buzzards - I've seen them taking the chicks - and on the top the skies were full of skylarks but you don't see many of them now either.

I can remember in the mid-50s a terrible flood in the valley. The Dane wasn't very wide down here and Macc Fisheries had just stocked it with fish. Lord Derby had had a big machine up on the moors cutting big gullies to drain it. There came a terrific thunderstorm which left the flats flooded with silt and the river twice as wide; it was ferocious. Charlie Brown had hencotes on his flat and he was trying to save his hens and was nearly swept away. Stephen Slack got a rope and saved him.

You used to see Charlie at eleven o'clock at night going up to his barn to milk his cows then he'd be up the next morning at six to milk again because he had to catch the milk wagon below Spring Head at nine o'clock. He went by pony and trap on a track over the fields. I used to go shooting rats with my air rifle at the Knar and many times I came home from there at two in the morning and Stephen would still be doing his jobs; they were great characters.

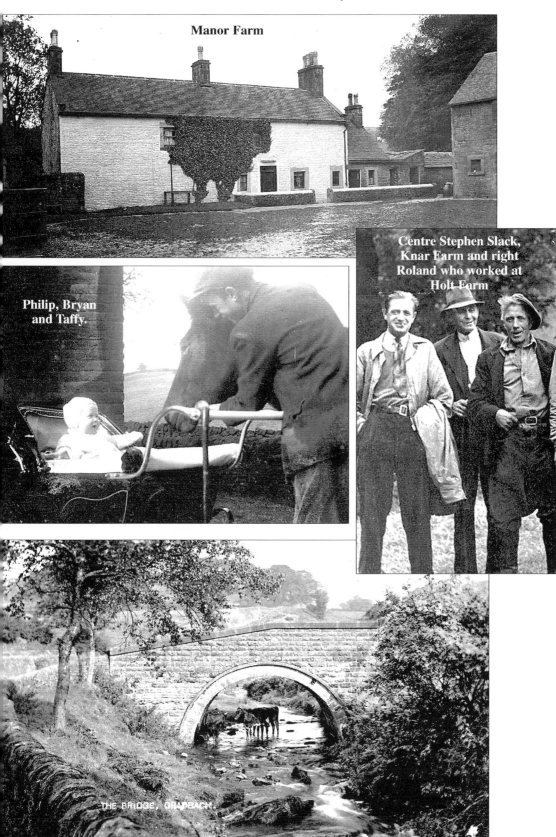

Manor Farm

Philip, Bryan and Taffy.

Centre Stephen Slack, Knar Farm and right Roland who worked at Holt Farm

THE BRIDGE, GRADBACH.

John Nadin

In wartime my dad, Ernest Nadin, John Hodgkinson and Ron Grindey were part of the team that felled Gradbach Wood by the Black Brook which joins the Dane at Forest Bottom. It was a massive wood which went right up to Roche End. What we knew as Swythamley Wood was on the other side. Then they felled Helmsley Wood on the Cheshire side of the Dane. That went all the way to Allgreave. It was all for the war effort.

John did the hauling out; he hauled it to Turn o' t' Rake near Sniddles from Gradbach Wood with an old Standard Fordson tractor. Helmsley Wood was taken through Helmsley onto the Wincle Road. Evans Bellhouse had the contract and Emlyn Philips was the manager. It was all done by axe and crosscut - no chainsaws then. There were a lot of hardwoods and some firs; virtually nothing was left. Later they felled the far piece of Swythamley Wood; they got as far as Castle Rocks; it was never replanted.

Dad was paid by Evans Bellhouse. He worked full time between milking the two cows and doing the hens but mother actually did most of that. He once got hurt, caught in belting between a stationary engine and the blade of the saw and was off work for a good while. The saw was for cutting it into lengths.

Mary Sigley

Gladys Downes and Mary and Daisy Sigley worked with the men. The men felled the trees and the women followed with axes then the trees were ready for towing out. Mary and Daisy were involved in the cutting up as well. Any timber that was left, that they didn't want, Paul Dodd who lived at Dane Cottage started getting that out. He took it up into a hut in the stone quarry on Bongs (Bangs) with an armoured car where he would cut it up then sell it.

When the job was finished dad went working in the woods at Chatsworth with Evans Bellhouse for a while till mother got fed up of him only being at home at weekends. He had a motor bike and would go on Sunday night and come back Friday night.

They got to keeping five cows at Greensytch and then mother started this hen farming. We had thousands - later on we used to hatch 1400 chickens a week in incubators. All free range in 20 odd hen cotes; Greensytch was covered with them. The chickens were sold for egg laying. There were Rhode Island Red and Light Sussex, some

pure and some crossed. White Leghorn/RIR cross, Black Leghorn/RIR cross, Brown Leghorn/RIR cross and some Game/RIR cross for the table. All in different cotes. The breeding stock cockerels were mainly bought in from Chivers at Cambridge with some from D H Bloor at Cheadle.

With being free range everything was healthy; we had no bother till later years when Coccidiosis started up. That seemed to be a new disease that came, perhaps brought by birds.

In a morning you had to check the incubators were filled with paraffin and clean the wicks and every night from 7 till 10 o'clock was spent turning eggs - 12 incubators with 150 eggs in each one. The eggs were marked with O on one side and 1 on the other. It was me and dad mainly; in the season from October until March or April we didn't have a night off.

In a morning we went round to feed them and check them. In the afternoon we took more feed round and collected the eggs and whoever drew the short straw went round at night to shut them up.

John with chicks

When I was 15 the electric came and we had to use £51 worth of electricity per year for five years and then you didn't have to pay for the line and them bringing it. So we had everything electric - two incubators that held 3,000 eggs each. We hatched all we wanted and sold any surplus to Hart Brothers at Pointon.

When my sister Mary was 15 she went and lodged at Rainow with Daisy and Norman Nadin, our relations. She was an apprentice at Stirlings Chicks at Walnut Tree Farm, Prestbury where she learned how to sex chicks. Then she travelled all over England working for them and doing ours as well.

The only trouble we had was with dogs. There were no foxes, badgers or magpies because Jack Beswick from Flash was gamekeeper. If you told him there was a fox about he'd wait days until he got him.

Dad got up to ten cows and then we built a new shippon and got up to 18. Frank and Annie Tunnicliffe at Manor milked 24 shorthorns and that was a big farm then. Freda and I had 30-40 Friesians including young ones. The churn wagon never came to our house; we took it all to the Manor with a donkey and cart or pony and cart and latterly with a van. But then as soon as the tanker started we were scuppered because he wouldn't come.

John

John and Mary

Walter Mountford lived at New House beyond Greensytch. He had two big Shire horses and him and Susie, his daughter, used to bowl the milk churns all the way to the Manor from there and the horses would be stood with their heads over the wall watching. Somebody said to Susie, 'That's hard work bowling those churns all that way' - there was a track because it was not a metalled road - and she replied, 'It's not so bad, it's a pound a dee.' That's what they were paid.

In the 1950s there was a terrible flash flood; we saw a wall of water coming down the valley. When it subsided we went down to the mill to look at the damage. It had washed away the stone basin which fed the mill race. As we got near to the mill building we heard a voice; we tried to open the door but it was wedged with debris. Eventually dad got it open and we looked in. Harold was floating around in a corn barrel but all he could say was, 'What will me dad say?'

At Greensytch

Edward Green, John Nadin,
Ann Green, Mary Nadin,

Ernest

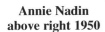
Annie Nadin
above right 1950

John and Mary

Mary and John

Guarding the pig!

Mary, John and Geoff Tunnicliffe and Jinny the donkey 1946.

Mary, Flash
May Queen
1950.

Mary

My Grandad, Sam Downes lived at Forest Bottom, near
Casters Bridge, in the early 1920s. It was afterwards
known as Shelley Cottage. From here he walked to
Swythamley where he was employed as a stone mason.
The rent was £6 a year.   Derek Riley

Millicent Downes at
Forest Bottom, c.1923

Late 1920s at the coal pit

**1932, Arthur Prince, Mary and Mr Sigley at
Gradbach Mill**

Bessie Worsley

I was born at Greens Farm, Gradbach in February 1929. My mother was Ann and she came from Litton. My dad, Joseph Sigley, worked a coal mine at Flash which he rented from the Harpur Crewe Estate. He was a hard man but he'd had to work hard; his father had died when he was about 12 and he went to live with his grandparents at Middlehills.

My oldest sister, Edith was 20 years older than me, then there was Joe, Gladys, Laurence and Teddy. But then dad was so cruel with my mother that they parted; he wouldn't let her take the children and eventually she came back because Teddy caught pneumonia. She came back to look after him but he died; he was only four. In the meantime dad had been seeing another woman from Flash and she had a child, Mary. My mother was also expecting and had Daisy about 8 weeks later. This woman didn't want Mary so mother had 2 babies to look after and when they went to school people used to ask, Why aren't you twins? and they used to get called for that. Then along came Florrie, then me, and then Harold and Cyril, so there were 10 of us.

There was no water on tap at all at Greens; it had to be fetched from a well down in the field for washing, cleaning and doing vegetables. For drinking and boiling the vegetables it was fetched in buckets from across the road down some steps.

We moved to the Mill House in 1931; there were 6 bedrooms there. It was also rented from the Harpur Crewe Estate. It was three storeys high and Dr Dakeyne had a surgery in the end bit. There were stone seats round the outside where people waited and Bachelors Buttons and other herbs grew which they used for medicine. The Dakeyne family had run the mill but it was never a success.

Mill House, Bessie and her Dad at the gate.

It was a very cold house; in the kitchen was a black lead range with side boiler and the pantry was at the back, underground, so it was always cold - you never needed a fridge; we just had a meat safe with netting on the front to keep the flies off. Underneath were big cellars with stone benches where we used to salt pigs.

We used to sell apples and oranges out of a box on the doorstep - anything to make money and they were a penny each. At weekends people used to come for tea and sandwiches like ramblers who'd been around Ludchurch. I remember as soon as we were old enough to handle cups and saucers we were washing up. Mum made scones as well and jam. We went bilberrying with a bucket and we had gooseberries in the garden and she made elderberry wine. I never could stand gooseberry jam; it was never sweet enough because sugar was hard to come by. Later, of course, were the watercress sandwiches; people loved them.

I didn't enjoy my childhood; my dad wouldn't let us do anything. We never had any new books, toys or anything; it was all work. I will say we never had any money but we were always well fed. We had a smashing mother but she put up with such a lot; he used to hit her and if things didn't go smoothly he'd whack everybody. We sat on a seat on a Sunday afternoon and weren't allowed to whisper or do anything. If we spoke he'd clap our heads together. Someone said he was like that because he'd been bought up strict. He was so bossy. If we were late home from school - it took us an hour to walk from Flash - we had rice pudding and we used to say the one who goes in first could have the skin off the pudding. We took it in turns because we knew we'd get hit so the one who went in first could scrape the dish.

We always hurried home at night but we called at Days opposite Barbers at Springhead. There were two lovely ladies and we knocked at the door to ask the time and they used to give us a lovely piece of cake. And we used to call at a little post box above Tunnicliffes and they used to leave the paper there which we took down every day. They gave us two pennies a week.

Near to Flash school, where the chapel and well is, was a little toffee shop which Sarah Jane kept. You went down three steps and you could get 10 aniseed balls for a penny or 2 liquorices and things like that which we divided between us. People were good to us in lots of ways because they knew what he was like.

When I was twelve years old I went to Leek School but it wasn't very nice; dad made me go in clogs with tips on which was alright at Flash but not at Leek because they marked the tiles. The teacher sent a letter to say I must not go in clogs but my dad wouldn't listen; he said all the others had gone in clogs so I used to take my Sunday shoes and change at the bottom of Goldsitch Moss where I got on the bus. I hid the clogs over the wall and covered them with bracken and leaves and hoped that no-one found them.

When dad finished at the coal mine he had the idea of the watercress. There were seven springs all coming out of the bank - beautiful, pure water. So with me two eldest brothers, we started to dig the beds out and built the clods round the sides. We started with four then made more as we went along and got more business till there were about twenty and the two canals. The water started in the canal and flowed through the beds; they all had to be slightly down so that the water was always flowing.

We got water cress roots from different places; someone let us have some and we

**Bessie, Florrie and
Harold**

**Bessie, Harold,
Florrie**

**Laurie and Joe
Gladys, Harold, Bessie,
Florrie, Mary, Daisy, Edith**

fetched some from below Pearls Farm and some from Nabbs. We planted willow trees round and next to where the car park is now, one of the beds grew dark, very strong cress - we thought it was because the water was tarry from coal.

As the roots established, when they flowered, we cut the flowers off. The beds had to be dug out once a year because they got weeds in so you weeded the bed and got it all clear and then took the flower heads and spread them about to drop seed and it made a new bed. The roots were mainly thrown away because it got full of water forget-me-not.

If the beds weren't weedy, you still had to dig them out every two years because the soil built up till the cress was out of the water so you pulled the cress out, dug the soil out and then set it all again. And you had to check the beds every day in case voles or water rats had made holes and let the water off so then you had to block the holes up.

Thursday was cutting day; it was a very cold job even with gloves on. You had shears to cut with and I've come back and haven't been able to undo the buttons on my coat. We finished at Christmas and should have started the second week in February but it was often too cold and snowy and there wasn't enough cress. It was usually just me and dad and we put the cress into boxes which we put in a deep pool until the next day.

So on Friday we took the cress down to the Mill House where we packed it on the kitchen table. We made bunches and put a rubber band round and a label on which said Krystal Spring. They were printed at Fred Hills in Leek. Then we packed the bunches into trays made from very thin wood woven together; they were strong but light. We put a dozen bunches one way then a dozen the other way, three dozen to a tray and perhaps take twelve dozen bunches altogether.

First he took it to Buxton with a tricycle, then he stood Macclesfield Market and when I was old enough I went with him; most of my brothers and sisters had left home so there was just me left. When I was eighteen he said I must go on my own; it was very hard work with the watercress on the front and I was only eight stone. I had a man's bike with a carrier on the front which we covered with sacking and I had to push it up to the Eagle and Child and then it was downhill for a bit then a walk up Long Dale and then downhill. I dropped some off at the Rose and Crown and stopped at various shops before getting to the market for 10 o'clock. We had a stall and were usually sold out by 12; 6d a bunch.

If I had any left Frank Reeves from the next stall took them and sold them because he knew what dad was like; he counted the money when I got back and he knew how many bunches and it all had to tally-- you didn't dare.....

After two years of going with that heavy bike Mr Hackett from Four Ways Garage said he'd take me; he charged ten shillings then I came back on the half past two bus to Clulow Cross and then walked back from there. It was a long way but my baskets were light with just a few things like sausages from Gaskills.

We had a few cows but dad decided he wanted Jerseys so he bought some and paid quite a lot of money for them. Dad and I did the milking by hand; the milk was so rich you could put a penny on it and it wouldn't sink. Mother made butter from it and every morning I used to take milk in a churn with the donkey and cart to Manor Farm where it was picked up. We had a Jack donkey called Jimmy and Ernest Nadin from Greensytch had a Jenny and sometimes Jimmy would go mad after her and take off so it was like a race. I once went over the bridge on two wheels and wondered how I would get round; I thought I'd hit the wall.

The watercress beds

Bessie and her Dad in the watercress

We did most of the work with the donkey - get the manure out and all. We mowed several meadows and crofts; we had an Allen Motor Scythe but sometimes got Frank Tunnicliffe to mow with horses then we had to turn it and ted it by hand and then fetch it with the donkey and cart. We put some in the loft at the Lodge Building and put some into the mill.

The 'Lodge' building

We used to plough a croft; we had a pony at one time and a hand plough. You'd take the weeds off, then the stones and then break the soil up with little harrows and then drill it. It was hard to keep the drills level because it was too much for the pony. I had to lead it and try to keep it straight but it was such a struggle and dad used to say, 'It's like a bloody dog's hind leg'. I've gone for my dinner in floods of tears and could hardly eat.

We reared heifer calves; we used to winter 6 or 7 in the Lodge Building. It was a lovely building; there were stalls for horses with lovely big mangers with racks and iron fasteners. When the mill was working, horses could be changed there which were carting the silk or they could stay overnight and there was a fireplace. Someone would stay there to look after them.

People used to store their carts in the mill building, Barbers and Tunnicliffes; it was a stone flagged floor but in part of it we made a silage pit. Then there was the waterwheel; it was very big, 96 pockets. It was taken away in wartime for scrap while I was at school.

At Top Middle Edge.

Gwyneth and Bessie mowing.

Bessie

At Manor Farm

Spring 1947

The bell went too; it had a lovely tone - I think it went to somewhere else on the estate.

We went to chapel on Sunday afternoon after Sunday school in the morning; Mr Goodwin and his two daughters, Daisy and Annie, used to teach and Mr Birchinall as well. There were some cottages on the way to Manor Farm known as Doublers Row. An old couple, Martha and her husband lived there. He chewed twist and she smoked a clay pipe. Dad used to collect insurance from them when he was young.

George Kirkham from the Eagle and Child came to kill the pig; he used to go round doing it for people. Down the hill from there was the Peg Inn. They said they couldn't get a license so they used to sell pegs and give a glass of beer away with them to get round it.

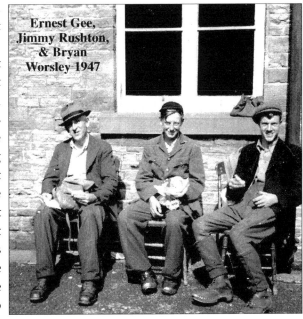

Ernest Gee, Jimmy Rushton, & Bryan Worsley 1947

Dad was so difficult; he didn't want me to have any male friends but I met Bryan who worked at Parks Farm and dad knew I wouldn't give him up so things went from bad to worse. He never spoke unless we were rowing or he was hitting me; it wasn't a happy life. I was glad to get away, just sorry for leaving my mum. We were married in December 1954 and went to live at Sniddles and it was lovely to get away to our own place even though it was in a bit of a mess when we took it. There were rats and dead pigs and when we looked in one shed, the bedding was so

Dad and Mr Parker

Gwyneth Pointon

Bessie

high, it had never been cleaned out, that they couldn't get the calves out. We had to get a hay knife and cut some away to get them out. It had really been let go but we got it straight and had three happy years there apart from when we lost a baby boy, but then Ann was born and later Margaret.

My brother Harold went home for a while but dad couldn't pay him enough to manage because he was married so they decided to have a sale and move to another property on the estate, Kennel Cottages near Melbourne. While they had gone to look at it there came a thunderstorm and a man who lived near us said what a mess there was. I wasn't allowed to go home after I married but

The new shippon at the Mill

Bryan and I went down to look. It was awful; the river had burst its banks and flooded the mill - everything was floating, the hay was washed away and there were little fish everywhere.

Major Young owned Sniddles and he wanted us to move to Dalbury Lees so that he could sell Sniddles so he built us a house there and we farmed for him but then he wanted us to go to Jersey and we didn't want to, so we moved back to Wincle and eventually we put in for Wildboarclough Post Office. We moved there in April 1963. We'd got 6 rooms and we had to sign a paper to look after Lord Derby's keepers and chauffeurs. Although it was hard work we had many happy years there.

Post Office, Wildboarclough

Hilda Mitchell

My Grandparents, Sampson and Ruth Kirkham went to Yorkshire where Grandad worked in the mines. He got hurt and they came back and took the Eagle and Child in 1919. It was a small farm and had just ceased being a pub. It was rented from Lord Derby and they also had the Rose and Crown Hill which made 60 acres altogether which they then bought when it came up for sale in the 1950s. As well as farming, Granny made tea for hikers.

Dad met my mother who was from Lower Greasley, Wincle and they married in 1939; I came along in 1942 and my brother John in 1944. Mum did the farming here while dad went around shearing, pig-killing, wall building and other farm work for local farmers. She kept hens, sold eggs, dressed poultry. There were a few cattle - one was milked for the house and we sold a few stirks at Flash Market in the autumn. I can remember walking up the New Road with them; it seemed that every gate was open and most walls had a gap in them!

When a cow needed the bull she was walked to Helmesley or Findlows or Birchenbooth; I can remember walking up there. I used to go shearing with dad sometimes; I remember going to Rushtons at The Holt. He used hand shears and taught me so I did a few hoggs. There were also a few pigs; dad sold the litters at weaning. The sows also had to be walked to where there was a boar locally then when my brother started driving he used to take them in the van.

We kept a horse, mainly to get manure out and to take stuff onto the other hill because it's nearly a mile away. Sometimes he had a load of lime and he fetched the rushes to thatch the stack. He used to scythe them into swathes and we had to keep them all the same way as we loaded them into the dobbin cart - the heads one way and the root ends the other. Then you had thatch string and he spent ages making thatch pegs.

Dad wore clogs and ironed them himself. Mum did all her own sewing and winter evenings were spent making rag rugs. In wartime a lady called Dorothy stayed with us because she was doing war work in the woods. She went home at weekends. Lots of couples came to stay for their honeymoon over the years too.

Granny continued doing pots of tea for hikers helped by Aunty Ada, her unmarried daughter who also lived here. There were more and more people and by the time we finished in 1990 there were more than we could cope with. Regulations came in and we needed separate facilities so we gave up. I carried on farming and my husband Alan went to work for Macclesfield Borough Council so it was history repeating.

The sign over the door which is cut in stone is from the crest of the Stanley family, the Lord Derbys, and comes from a legend from several centuries ago. Sir Thomas de Lathom was an elderly but wealthy knight of Lancashire. He wanted a son so fathered an illegitimate one but how could he bestow his wealth on him? He is said to have had the child left in a wood where an eagle had its nest and fetched his wife to accidently discover him. She concluded that it was the will of God that they should adopt the child for their heir and he was baptised Oskatell de Lathom and his daughter is said to have married Sir John Stanley. S.H.

Thatching

1930s
George Kirkham shearing

George

John, Uncle Bob and Dad

Mum and Dad 1940

Brew time for snow ridders at Eagle & Child. George Kirkham on left

Mrs Downes on left from Gradbach Old Hall

Learning muckspreading

Grandma Kirkham, Dad, Mum Auntie Ada, John and Hilda

At the Eagle and Child

Mr Bell from Midgely Gate Farm getting muck out at Eagle & Child with George, John and Hilda. Mid 1950s.

Ada

Hilda and John, Hetty and Stanley Mellor c.1950

Granny with Ann and Ada   **Right: Ada**

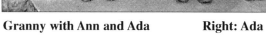

Vera Barber

I was born at Pearls Farm, Allgreave in 1930. My mother's parents went to the farm from Sutton renting it from Lord Derby. My father George came from Quarnford and when he married my mother, Mabel, they went to live there. They milked around 20 Shorthorn cows and kept sheep.

Vera

I had a happy childhood and walked to Wincle School. My grandma Swindells played the organ at Allgreave Chapel for 60 odd years. It was a pedal organ and when she started to play at age 12 she struggled to reach the pedals. When she finished I took over. My cousin who lived nearby at Midgeley gave me a few lessons; she was a good player. I played regularly until I retired to Sutton 25 years ago and then the minister used to come and pick me up to play at times.

I went to Gradbach Chapel Sunday School at 6 years of age. There was a very good attendance and Mrs Daisy Nadin used to teach us. When she left Gradbach the older ones of us took it over. There would be in the teens of children; the younger ones did their own amusements and the older ones had lessons from the scriptures. We had a happy time but a few that came were a problem; it was generally one or two families that came in from away who were disruptive. I tried to be strict but it didn't always work.

It was Sunday School at Gradbach in the morning and Allgreave service in the afternoon. I gave it up when I moved but went back to Gradbach to play the organ about once a month and for special services.

THE BRIDGE & CHAPEL, GRADBACH.

Doreen Dean

I live at Allgreave Farm where I was born in 1945 though during my married life I have lived at Midgeley Farm. My grandparents Sidney and May Mason lived here and my mother Doris was born and lived here until she was 82. Before Allgreave Chapel was built services were held here in the front room I was told. Then John Wheelton, who

Mrs Findlow

lived here at that time, gave the piece of land for the chapel to be built on in 1871. I was taken to the chapel as a baby and attended until it closed in October 2000. It was in the Macclesfield Circuit and not registered for weddings but we had several christenings; my boys were christened there.

The regular congregation was 8 or 9; my husband Reg was a member and also at Walker Barn. We had an Anniversary service in June and a harvest festival when the chapel would be full. There would be a harvest sale afterwards and the auctioneer was Bill Dean and later Frank Hooley. We also had either a cricket or rounders match held at Midgeley Farm. It was always well attended with local people and people from Macclesfield from some of the other churches.

When we had the Centenary service we had refreshments afterwards in a wooden shed in the top garden here. Local ladies helped; Mabel and Vera Barber, Alice Hooley, Irene Belfield, Beryl Nield, my mother, Doris Findlow. The Rose and Crown gave a cake; they were always very helpful at the pub.

The chapel wall was knocked down quite a few times by wagons so dad approached the council and said that he would give a piece of land on the other side of the road to widen it so they widened it quite a lot and built a new wall and he had an agreement which has just lapsed that the council would maintain the new wall and down roadside.

In the last few years before the chapel closed we joined with Gradbach which was in the Leek Curcuit and they came to us for one service in the month and we went to them for another.

On the farm here my father, Frank Findlow, kept dairy cows and sheep. When I left school he added poultry which became my job. We had three big deep litter sheds and some hens in the barn above the road too. In the granary near the house we had day old chicks under lamps. I did the hens, collected the eggs and washed any that needed it and packed them ready to be collected by the packing station.

In the barns below the road were about 30 milkers and another of my jobs was to carry the cans of milk down the shippon to where the churns were in the corn place and tip the milk through a sieve and when the milk was cooled to wheel the churns across the road to where the wagon picked them up. The driver had to lift the churns onto the wagon; it went to Staniers Dairy at Lyme Green.

The woods at Allgreave and Midgeley are very old we have been told and haven't changed in my lifetime. There have always been lots of deer especially in the wintertime. Dad used to go fishing down at the river then he let it to the Prince Albert Fishing Club at Macclesfield; they had it right until this last year. They used to stock it with fish at one time. After the flood of 1989 the riverbank altered a lot. In some places it is wider and in others steeper. There were brown trout left out in the field and my boys went throwing some of them back in.

Alice Hooley, Doris Findlow, Irene Belfield, Beryl Neild. Doreen Dean with Paul and Alistair. Centenary Celebrations

Allgreave

ALLGREAVE METHODIST CHURCH
(MACCLESFIELD CIRCUIT)

Centenary Celebrations

Saturday and Sunday
June 12th and 13th
1971

Saturday, June 12th

Don't miss the

" Saturday Rendezvous "

—Thanksgiving Meetings at 3 and 6-30 p.m.
in Mr. Findlow's field (by chapel)
—if wet, in barn.

Meetings led by

Rev. HOWARD BELBEN, M.A., B.D.
(Principal of Cliff College)

supported by Students from the College
with musical items
and
Over Alderley Methodist Church Band

Buffet Teas (Adults 15p, Children 10p)
from 4-30 p.m.

*(To help with catering, please purchase your tea ticket, if
possible, prior to June 12th from Mr. G. R. Dean,
Midgley Farm, Allgreave.)*

Sunday, June 13th

Centenary Services
in the Chapel

2-30 p.m.
Preacher: Rev. ERIC CHALLONER
(Alderley Edge)

6-30 p.m.
Preacher: Rev. HENRY GREAVES, LL.B.
(Superintendent Minister)

Soloist: Miss F. E. SWINDELLS
(Macclesfield)

MESSAGE FROM THE SUPERINTENDENT MINISTER

*So Allgreave Chapel reaches its 100th birthday.
Built to house the local Methodist Society and serve the
community in Christ's name in the middle years of
Queen Victoria's reign, it still maintains its witness.*

*As Superintendent Minister, I am delighted to bring
greetings and congratulations to the Society from the
Circuit, and I know many others outside the Circuit would
wish to be associated with me in the expression of these
sentiments. We thank God for all that has been
accomplished here, under His providence, over the years
and pray His rich blessing on those who represent the
cause today.*

**Old view of church
before the road was
changed**

**Wincle
Church
c.1910**

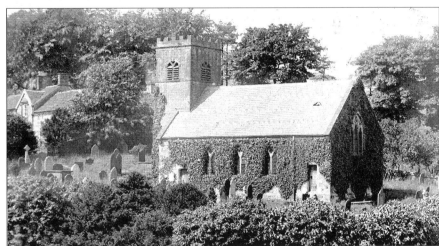

**Old Crown Inn c.1900
Proprietor Nathaniel Bagshaw**

Norman Goodwin

My grandad Philip Sidney Goodwin was born at Back o' th' Cross below Flash into a big family. When he was 11 he went to live with an uncle in Macclesfield who had a milk round and he had to deliver milk and then go to school in Sutton. When he left school he went to work for Uncle Leonard Buxton at Henbury again delivering milk. They used to milk three times on a Sunday and deliver milk in the middle of the day.

He used to tell us about a brewery in Macclesfield where he had to fetch grains from. He had to get in the vat and throw the brewers grains out and they went down a chute into the cart at the bottom. One day he got out and the horse had gone and all the grains were on the floor. He went looking for the horse and a policeman on point duty in front of the town hall was holding it. He had to take it back and load his grains up.

Sydney Goodwin and Harry Brown 1903

He went working at Hammerton for Uncle Henry Hine where he met Dora Hine. She was from Oxhay, Meerbrook, and had been farmed out to Uncle Henry and his wife as a child because they had no children. They were getting fond of one another so grandfather was packed off. He went to Fallows at Bosley for four years so he had to trudge back to Hammerton from there to court grandma; they weren't going to be stopped. Some relation of grandfather called Mitchell went to Canada and they sent for him to go but Dora hid the letter until after they were married.

He got the tenancy of a farm at Langley from Whistons Print Works - Ridgegate Farm behind the Leather Smithies pub. He got put off that farm by Macclesfield Corporation because they wanted to plant all the land with trees to buffer the reservoirs so as Uncle Henry wanted to retire, Grandad and Grandma moved back to Hammerton.

They made Cheshire Cheese which was sold in Macclesfield. They used to take it to the Co-op but they weren't getting the full price; the Co-op said the cheese was second grade. So grandad went off to see them. 'What's wrong with this cheese?' 'It's too soft - not crumbly enough.' They said. He said, 'I can soon make it crumbly; I can skim some cream off and make some butter.' 'Oh no Mr Goodwin, we've got customers for your cheese.' So he said it would have to be first grade price then.

There was a cheese room which later we used to sleep in. The cheese was stored in it. If there was too much he would sell some to Fred Adams who at one point didn't fetch it for a month. He sent a man to fetch it when he knew grandad would be at Leek on a Wednesday but grandad had left word that he couldn't have it because cheese loses weight every week. Fred Adams was very annoyed and threatened to take him to court.

When father was young, at weekends they used to send the milk down to these uncles who retailed milk. Grandfather had a motor car very early on; he was one of the

**Grandparens
Dora and
Sydney**

**Philip
Sydney Goodwin,
Henry Hine, George
Shufflebottom, at
Hammerton Farm
c.1910**

first in Wincle and they used to load the milk into the back of the car. Dad had to go with him because the car couldn't get up Barlow Hill loaded; it was too high geared. So when it stopped, father had to jump out and put a scotch under the wheel then grandfather let it run back onto the scotch and then it could go on again a bit further. After a few times it could go on then dad could jump out and run back home.

Grandad was always gone with the gun, shooting or foxing. He was also on the War Ag Committee and a county councillor at Macclesfield with responsibility for repairs to roads and bridges. He was also a magistrate and was on Macclesfield Rural District Council from 1933 to 1974.

When my parents married they lived in one end of the house then in 1946 they moved down to Bartomley Farm. Poysers were there before and grandma bought it with a legacy. The Swythamley agent was sent to buy it because they wanted the fishing on the river. He thought it was enough money so stopped bidding and

Grandma Goodwin bought it. Sir Philip went mad when he got back. He said he had told him to go and buy it, not bid for it.

Dad took 12 cows from Hammerton though half were three papped, and 50 pullets. He went back to milking them by hand and had a van to take the milk up. He had to back up the lane because it was lower geared in reverse.

I had three brothers and as lads we used to go off for the day and mum wouldn't know exactly where we were. Hogg Clough is between Bartomley and Mellor Knowle and there was a deep pool where the brook there joined the River Dane which we knew as otter hole. We were always told never to go near it.

There used to be a hut down that way and a Mr Fred Hartley came to it at weekends. He had a mill in Stalybridge and it was his getaway - he owned it. When my father badly injured his foot with a motorbike chain, Mr Hartley was very good with him and used to take him to the infirmary. We roamed around the Dane and I can remember Folly Mill with the roof on and the floors in although it was derelict. We used to go in it.

Old John Goodwin from Back Dane told me that German POWs fetched timber out of Back Forest Wood. There was a machine dragging timber out which got off the track. It was stuck for several days and then this German POW said, I can get it out. So as they were beaten they let him have a go. He paid out all the winch rope and they tightened it up then he went and swung on the rope and got it bouncing and it got the thing out. After that they put him in charge of getting the timber out and transporting it.

I remember the '47 blizzard. Dad couldn't get out of the yard at Bartomley the top way so he pulled a wall down and went round to get out with his milk on a sledge and they took it to the Ryles Arms to meet the lorry. That was also a meeting place for groceries. He said that once he and Jim Brunt walked for bread to the Ryles Arms in a blizzard but they were nearly made away and wouldn't do that again.

Grandfather retired and moved into one end of the house at Hammerton in 1949 and dad farmed with Jim Hine, my father's second cousin who was reared with him. His family were from Nettlebeds and were wiped out with TB in three months. Three children were left and my grandparents as Godparents took Jim in to live with them.

Hammerton was originally called Hommerton but my grandma changed it and the road called Rabbit Bank went up to Banktop which Aunty Nellie changed to Hill Top.

I went to Wincle School; teachers Mrs Malkin, Mrs Cleaver and Mrs Roberts though there were only nine of us at one stage. The vicar was Mr Elliot who liked a drink. Dad was a churchwarden along with Harold Shufflebottom. Granthams were at Mellor Knowle; we were always told that they owned Belle Vue in Manchester. Mellor Knowle had been completely knocked down and rebuilt because of dry rot. They quarried stone from the back of Mellor Knowle Farm which he also owned. The old three legs was still there from loading the stone and that was where Horace Whittaker started Whittakers Lorries. He lived at The Old Smithies and bought a 30 cwt lorry to cart materials for building the house. He built Four Ways Garage and pumps. Hacketts had the pumps when I was a lad.

We had a good youth club down at Danebridge Chapel; there were about 20 of us and met on Monday nights. We went to Switzerland on a trip; Brian Page from Woodlands was in charge.

Wincle Fete c.1950

Tom Jones, postman from Pringle Cottage, back right in hat.

The vicar is Stuart Elliot

Wincle Fete 1961

'Little Miss Tunnicliffe' 1923

Wincle School c.1910.

Late 1920s Bus trip to Belle Vue
Front: Dennis Mayer, Ruth Gibson, Millicent Downes, Fred Titterton, Arthur Beresford, Wilfred Goodwin,
Tommy Whittaker, Walton Wyche, Evelyn Hooley, Lillian Downes, Mary Goodwin
nd: Tom Poole, Jim Hooley, Eric Goodwin, Joe Aidley, Doris Mason, Ivy Whittaker, Mabel Mayer, Ethel Goodwin
On back row are Sam Gibson, Dora Goodwin, Molly Aidley

Wincle School c.1932
Doris Mason, - -, - -, Mrs Grantham, Milly Downes
Front 2nd from left Lily Downes

**Wincle School 1953
Coronation**

**Mr and Mrs Tunnicliffe
Wincle Fete 1929**

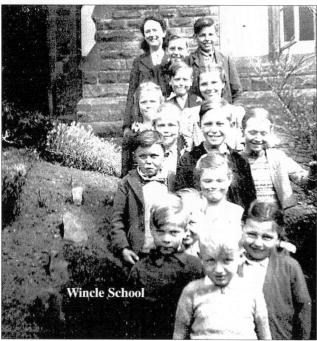

Wincle School

Bernard Brunt baling

Jim Brunt

**Below:
Jim and Phyllis Brunt 1952
Lane House Farm**

Jess Tunnicliffe

**Jim Brunt, Vicar Lankey,
Jess Tunnicliffe mid-1960s**

**Mole catching demonstration
Wincle Grange 1950s**

**Nellie Tunnicliffe and
Phyllis Brunt early 1960s**

**Bernard Brunt
early 1950s**

Graham Corbishley

I have lived at Lower Greasley since 1950. It was a sixty three acre rented farm at that time. My parents were Frank and Winnie and they milked 20 cows and kept a few pigs. They had a little grey Fergy that year to do the farm work instead of a horse. I had a happy childhood helping on the farm and playing in the valley along with my sister Marjorie.

The woods at Mare Knowles and Higher Greasley had been cut down and they went to Manchester; I thought a lot went for firewood. Our landlord wanted to fall all our woods but when he couldn't he sold the farm and dad bought it in 1952. Dad sold a few odd trees then. Later on he bought adjoining land to make 120 acres.

Timber.

TO BE SOLD BY AUCTION,

At the House of Mr Goodwin, known by the Sign of the Angel, in Macclesfield, in the County of Chester, on Monday the 1st of April, 1793, between the Hours of Four and Six in the Afternoon, either together, or in separate Lots; subject to such Conditions as will then and there be produced,

THE following very valuable Lots of TIMBER, now standing and growing on a Tenement or Farm, called Hawkes Lee, within Wincle, in the said County, in the Tenure or Occupation of Joseph Lomas.

Lot 1st. Five Hundred Oaks, and One Hundred and Fifty nine Cyphers, all regularly marked, and numbered with Scribes, beginning at No. 1. and ending at No. 501.

Lot 2d. Five Hundred Oaks, and One Hundred and Fifty-nine Cyphers, also regularly marked and numbered with Scribes, beginning at No. 501, and ending with No. 1000.

Lot 3d. One Hundred and Seventeen Ash, Sixteen Birch, One Asp, One Hundred and Forty-eight Alder, and One Hundred and Eighty Cyphers, regularly marked and numbered together, with Scribes, beginning with No. 1, and ending with No. 282.

N. B. The above Timber is remarkably well Grown, and suitable for Carpenters, Joiners, Ship-wrights, and Coopers use; and grows within six Miles of Macclesfield, six of Congleton, seven of Leek, and nine of Buxton, and within one Mile of the several Turnpike Roads leading from Macclesfield, Leeke, and from Congleton to Buxton.

The said Joseph Lomas will shew the Timber to any Person desirous of viewing the same; and for further Particulars apply to Mr. Henry Cherry, of Sutton, near Macclesfield, or to Mr. Ridgway and Son, Attornies, in Manchester.

Lower Greasley

There were always peewits on the top field but you don't see them now; I don't know if its because of all the buzzards and we are alive with badgers when there used to be none. We only saw deer after the late 60s. Dad used to catch a lot of trout in the Shell Brook; one summer he had about 200 good sized ones but it's been washed out these last few years and you don't see the big ones come up now. There are quite a lot of herons; my dad didn't like them.

It's an old property going back to the 1600s and there's a brick barn; my dad said they used to make the bricks in the valley.

CAPITAL TIMBER.

TO BE SOLD BY AUCTION,

At the house of Mr. Braddock, the Red Lion Inn, in Leek, in the county of Stafford, on Monday the 12th day of January next, precisely at four o'clock in the afternoon, subject to such conditions as will be then produced ;

A Quantity of full grown OAK, ASH, ELM, ALDER, and BIRCH, growing in Heaton, in the parish of Leek, and in Wincle, in the county of Chester, in the undermentioned Lots :—

CHESHIRE.
LOT 1.—*Rye Croft Wood.*

115 Oaks, from No. 204 to No. 318, both inclusive, and 16 ciphers.
6 Ash and 4 ciphers.
2 Alders and 3 ciphers.

8 Trees, from No. 114 to No. 121, both inclusive.
LOT 2.—*White Lee Clough.*

59 Oaks, from No. 319 to No. 377, both inclusive, and 5 ciphers.
14 Ash and 6 ciphers.
9 Elm and 2 ciphers.

23 Trees, from No. 122 to No. 144, both inclusive.
LOT 3.—*Little Fern Eyes and Great Fern Eyes.*

324 Oaks, from No. 810 to No. 1133, both inclusive, and 14 ciphers.
14 Birch and 7 ciphers.
28 Alders and 8 ciphers.
16 Ash and 12 ciphers.
1 Sycamore.

59 Trees, from No. 266 to No. 321, both inclusive.
STAFFORDSHIRE.
LOT 4.—*Middle Part of Paper Mill Wood.*

156 Oaks, from No. 563 to No. 718, both inclusive, and 59 ciphers.
9 Birch and 20 ciphers.
3 Ash and 2 ciphers.

12 Trees.
LOT 5.—*Lower Part of Paper Mill Wood.*

91 Oaks, from No. 719 to No. 809, both inclusive, and 49 ciphers.
1 Alder.
3 Ash and 3 Alders.

4 Trees, from No. 262 to No. 365, inclusive.

The Oak is of large dimensions, suitable for Ship timber, building, and cleft ; and the Ash, Alder, Birch, and Elm, are very large and good. The situation of the lots is about six miles from the Leek Wharf of the Grand Trunk Canal, and contiguous as well to the road from Leek to Macclesfield, as from Congleton to Buxton.

GEORGE PICKFORD, of Wincle, will shew the lots; and particulars may be had at the Office of Messrs. CRUSOS and COUPLAND, Leek.

Leek, 12th December, 1833.

TIMBER.
TO BE SOLD BY TICKET,

At the house of Mrs. Turnock, the GOLDEN LION INN, in RUSHTON, in the county of Stafford, on Thursday, the 29th day of November, 1838, at five o'clock in the afternoon, subject to such conditions as will be then produced ;

THE following lots of TIMBER, growing at Barley Ford, in Wincle, in the county of Chester.

LOT 1.—Ninety-five Alders scribed from 1 to 95 inclusive, and 32 Cyphers ; 17 Elms, scribed from 1 to 17 inclusive, and 25 Cyphers ; 9 Beech, scribed from 1 to 9 inclusive, and 6 Cyphers ; 19 Birch, scribed from 1 to 19 inclusive, and 35 Cyphers ; 2 Asp, scribed from 1 to 2 inclusive.

LOT 2.—Seventy-two Ash, scribed from 1 to 72 inclusive. 73 Ash Cyphers.

LOT 3.—Thirty-seven Oaks, scribed from 1 to 37 inclusive ; 18 Oak Cyphers.

LOT 4.—Sixteen Oaks, scribed from 38 to 53 inclusive. 35 Spruce, scribed from 1 to 35 inclusive.

LOT 5.—A quantity of Scotch Firs, (felled) and Post-wood.

The above Timber is all coppice. The Oak and Ash are of very excellent quality.

Barley Ford is situate near Rushton, half way between Leek and Macclesfield.

Mr. GEORGE BULLOCK, the tenant, will shew the timber. Any further information may be had from Mr. JOHN LEECH, Wall Bridge Farm, near Leek.

**Above:
Mum, Graham & Marjorie,
with evacuees Peter and Percy Sovery**

**Graham
and John
Sovery**

**Mr and Mrs
Sovery. Mr &
Mrs Corbishley
behind**

Annie Turnock

I was born at Mareknowles in 1930. Phyllis Tunnicliffe from Wood Cottage brought the midwife to me mother. We grew up there through the 1930s and 40s. There was no electric; mother baked all our own bread and made cheese and butter. She had a hard life. We had a good garden; I used to grow peas and Dorothy grew celery.

We started selling milk in 1944. We had in the teens of cows in three shippons, all milked by hand. Dad took the churns with the horse and float to the top of Dumbers. He had some starvins. He'd come back rubbin' his hands; it were rough over top to Barbers road end. 1947 was the worst; they dropped hay at Barbers and then we had fetch it with sledge. We lost quite a few cattle and some horses; we couldn't get enough feed to 'em but we got some compensation. Dorothy and me went shopping in Macclesfield. We walked up the hill, then down the fields near Minnend lane to the main road where we thumbed a lift. We came back on the train and carried the groceries from Bosley Station.

I used to fetch the cows in early in a morning then get my brother Fred off to work on the timber job. He worked for Evans and Bellhouse - they felled all them trees at Barleyford.

Logging at Barleyford 1942-3

The famous canal pioneer and engineer James Brindley and his family spent a time at Mareknowles in the early 1700s. He was born in 1716 at Tunstead in Derbyshire but his family were yeoman farmers from the Leek area where they also lived at Lowe Hill afterwards. He is known locally for the Brindley Mill in Leek and was a pioneer in the early days of canal building for the technique of contouring which although it made canals longer minimised earthmoving in the days when canals were dug and constructed by hand. He is also credited with devising the way of preventing the canal from leaking by puddling clay.   S.H.

'My grandparents, Sam and Emmy Beardmore lived at Dumkins. My mum, Christine was four when they moved to Gun End in 1954. Mum said that it was haunted and my uncle Ted used to say that the ghost would pick the poker up and poke the fire.'

Clive Grindey

Dumkins was built with cruck frames and thought to date back to 15thC. It was pulled down around 1980.   S.H.

Photo taken 1980 - Josie, Clive and Adrian Hambleton

Valuable Oak, Ash, Beech, and other Timber.

TO BE SOLD BY TICKET,

At the house of Mr. Holmes, the Macclesfield Arms Inn and Hotel, in Macclesfield, in the county of Chester, on Wednesday the 9th. day of December, 1835, precisely at three o'clock in the afternoon:

THE following Valuable LOTS of TIMBER of large dimensions, growing on lands in Wincle, in the county of Chester :—

Lot 1.—Twenty-two Oaks, numbered from 1 to 22; 13 Larch Timber, very large, numbered 1 to 13; 74 Spruce Timber, very large, numbered 1 to 74; 5 Scotch Fir Timber, numbered 1 to 5; 33 Cyphers.

Lot 2.—Seventeen Oaks, numbered from 23 to 39; 7 Ash, numbered from 1 to 7; 68 Spruce Timber, large, numbered from 75 to 142; 24 Cyphers.

Lot 3.—Twenty-three Oaks, numbered from 1 to 23; 12 Ash, numbered from 1 to 12; 39 Larch Timber, very large, numbered from 1 to 39; 98 Spruce Timber, very large, numbered from 1 to 98; 38 Cyphers.

Lot 4.—Twenty Oaks, numbered from 1 to 20; 18 Ashes, numbered from 1 to 18; 5 Alders, numbered from 1 to 5; 2 Birches; 8 Larches, large, numbered from 1 to 8; 70 Spruce, large, numbered from 1 to 70; 3 Scotch Firs, and 12 Cyphers.

Lot 5.—Eleven Oaks, numbered from 1 to 11; 3 numbered from 1 to 3; 1 Alder, and 1 Birch; 36 Timber, numbered from 1 to 36; 14 Scotch Fir, numbered from 1 to 14.

Lot 6.—Seven Oaks, numbered from 1 to 7; 5 Ashes, numbered from 1 to 5; 30 Beech Timber, large, numbered from 1 to 30; 24 Scotch Firs, numbered from 1 to 24; 10 large Spruce, numbered from 1 to 10.

The above Timber is scribe marked, and from its great length, straightness, and mature growth, is well worth the particular attention of timber merchants. The Larch and Spruce Trees are the finest in this part of the country, and would make excellent masts for flats and other vessels. The whole of the Lots are growing upon an estate in Wincle, belonging to Mr. Shufflebotham, who will show them to purchasers. The Timber is situated within two and a half miles of the Macclesfield Canal, within five miles of Macclesfield, and seven of Congleton, and lies contiguous to good roads in every direction. There are persons in the neighbourhood who will be happy to contract to lay the Timber down at any place, within a reasonable distance, for a moderate compensation, and some of them have been accustomed to falling and peeling oak, and understand the management of bark.

Further particulars may be had from Mr. SHUFFLE-BOTHAM, of Wincle aforesaid; or at the office of Messrs. BROCKLEHURST and BAGSHAW, in Macclesfield aforesaid.

N. B.—A large quantity of Clog and Turning Wood is ready for sale by Private Treaty, on the above estate.

Derek Riley

I was born at Number 3, Chapmans Row, Wincle in 1947. My Mum and Dad, George and Millicent Riley lived there for a while. As a lad Dad lived at Thornyleigh Green and because there were enough men working on the farm, he was called up in 1939. At some point during the war he was in hospital in Jerusalem and Sir Philip got to hear of it so he went to see him and offered him a job as soon as the war was over. His first job was shift work drying grass in the drying shed in the park.

There was always a problem with water running through our cottage. Mum told me that it came down the road and then ran through like a river. Sir Philip came down one day; he had a doctor staying with him and they said, 'We can't have you living like this with a baby. So he got onto the council and said, 'My men will work with you but I want it doing now.' They dug out at the back, put fresh drains in and concreted it. Sir Philip got that job done.

They moved here to number 2. Below here was the wash house where before my time all the row did their washing. There was a chimney, a fire and a boiler and Dad lit it in a morning. Mum and Dad both worked at Swythamley; Dad as an estate worker and Mum worked in the house every morning of the week including Sundays. Michael Goldman picked her up in a morning in a tiny blue wagon with Molly Aidley from Mount Pleasant Farm and sometimes Lily Mountfort, my aunt and he brought them back at lunchtime. Michael was Sir Philip's batman; when he didn't come the butler, Gerry Garrard came. He committed suicide in the stables in 1963 after domestic problems. Mum had been in the Red Cross during the war for about 5 years. She lived in at the hall which became a convalescent home mainly for American soldiers.

Dad was a beater on the shoots and I went from the age of nine. It was on the Roches and Gun Moor; heavy going across the moors - hard work but I enjoyed it. It was a grand grouse shoot. We used to sit outside Shawside for dinner. We had our sandwiches and some of the shooters would come and shake hands with us. I remember

Chapman's Row
c.1920

Dane Bridge Dane Valley 369-16

shaking hands with Lord Scarsdale and the
Duke of Westminster who at the time were the
richest men in the country. This was in the late
50s. Once in the 60s we were beating and the
gamekeeper then, either Maurice Bishop or Ron
Hancock, came running down to us shouting,
Stop! We're driving more wallabies than grouse.
He wasn't very happy that day. Right into the
70s if I went for a walk in the evening towards
Ludchurch I'd often see two or three wallabies.

I went to Wincle School - walked up
every day along with others that I met on the
bridge here; Heaths and later Mitchells from
Back Dane. I can't remember missing a day
for bad weather because the teacher, Mrs
Roberts lived there at the school. Pupils
walked down Barlow Hill from Four Ways
area and they did go home early if it was bad.

**Mary Lizzie Downes of Tolls Farm
coming up to the well, 1935**

There were 30-35 children at that time and usually one teacher; occasionally Mrs Malkin
helped out.

Mrs Grantham lived at Mellor Knowle; her parents were Jennisons who used to
own Belle Vue Zoo. A previous resident, Mrs Alsop had a dispute with Sir Philip's
father over the new bridge and road which involved raising the road behind Chapmans
Row. He then built another storey onto the Row to block the view and placed a
windvane on the post office chimney depicting a witch. The windvane is still there.

Mum used to work for Granthams in the afternoon; she used to go through the door
in the wall and up through the gardens. I used to go up and play too. Bagstones was
another place where Mum used to work and Dad too for Lady Brocklehurst, Sir Philip's
mother. She gave me a tray with nursery rhymes on.

I used to go doing farm work in the buildings there for Roger Griffiths. He milked
about 12-15 cows and I used to go up in a morning before I went to school to get the

milk and while I was there I'd go
across the fields to feed the hens
then bring back some milk in a
bucket with a lid on and a pint
ladle for The Ship and one or two
other places. Then call at the shop
for an ounce of Digger or twist for
Roger as I went up to school or to
get the school bus and drop it off
for him. In later years when
Dronfields were there, their son
started a restaurant in the farm
buildings where they sold

**Middle: Mary Lizzie Downes, right, Lady Lee Brocklehurst,
Sir Philip's sister, 1972 .**

Mellor Knowle

Right: Post Office Danebridge

Below:
George and Millicent Riley with Philip Mountfort and Derek Riley. In front Doreen Mountfort, Gillian Riley and Sylvia Mountfort

Mrs Beardmore and George Belfield mid 1950s

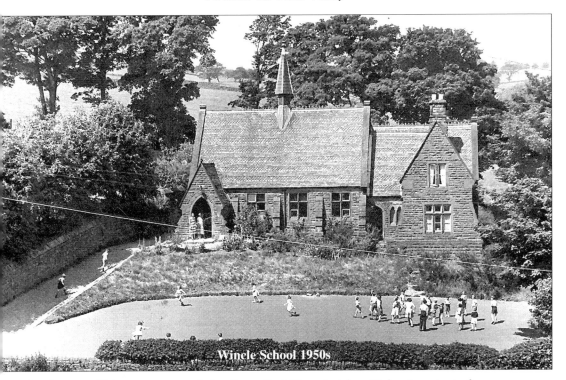

Wincle School 1950s

smoked trout. This was around the time that Danebridge Fisheries started up.

There was no road to Pingle Cottage and when I was a kid Tom Jones the postman lived there. He walked from the post office here up as far as Wildboarclough almost to the Cat and Fiddle and on the other side almost to where the tower is. He had a withered arm from shrapnel damage in the First World War and he used to tuck the post under his arm. He used to go to the Ship every night for a few pints and then you could hear him walking down the alleyway back to the Pingle.

Richardsons kept the shop in the early 50s then Sam Errock followed by the Buchanans. They did a lot of work in the village; Keith Buchanan took all the lads under his wing and we had cricket at Wincle Grange. We had nets up there and he took us to Test Matches at Old Trafford. There were concerts at chapel; Mrs Buchanan was involved in those. She went to the cash and carry every Thursday and had orders from the village which she made up when she got back. She employed staff because she was so busy. They left in the mid 60s and the shop closed in the late 70s.

We went to the Sunday school in the chapel regularly. We had three teachers; Sidney Gibson, Jack Allen and Marjorie Brunt. I think there were 30 of us there at one time. Grandma used to light the

Buchanan family 1965

Above:
The wire rope bridges

Tolls Farm

boiler and stoke up; she was always worried about having it warm enough on a Sunday so when we were living at Mount Pleasant, if I'd been out on a Saturday night, I'd go down at maybe 2.00am and stoke up so that she didn't have to go down first thing in the morning. When the coke arrived, it was a wagon load tipped outside by the bottom door and dad and I had to get it in with wheelbarrows, a long and dusty job! There were laurels all around which dad and I cut every year too.

I spent a lot of time in the woods; mum could remember the wire bridges and people using them especially the one below Bearda. I remember the Hanging Stone Wood being felled in the 50s and replanted with conifers. I used to go in there collecting sticks for my Grandma, Lizzie Downes who lived at Ashmount Cottage. When we came home from school we used to go up for a ride on the caterpillar tractor that was pulling the timber out.

The favourite place for picnicking was by the river below Tolls Farm here. Every weekend it was like Blackpool. You'd always see fishermen on the Dane, either from Prince Albert or Macclesfield Fly Fishers. You don't see as many nowadays. I used to tickle trout and then we used to light a fire and cook them. I remember dad replacing the fish ladders when they had been washed away in a flood.

In the 50s my grandma's half sister lived at Tolls Farm and I went there in a morning for a jugful of Jersey cream for my porridge. They had a mixture of cows that they milked by hand and kept the Jersey's milk for themselves. They left in 1958 and when Pyes lived there they had turkey cotes in the field; long ones that stretched half way down.

There were parties at Christmas in the Hall for workers and their families; I remember a conjuror every time and the last Tenant's party was in 1972 in the Tenant's Hall. That was the night that Michael died.

In the late 1960s there was a couple living at Pingle Cottage who were growing cannabis in the garden. Someone reported them and they said they were growing it to put in their hot pot hence the headline in the *News of the World*: Hot Pot Cottage. Apparently they were buying jelly babies in bulk from the Post Office, hollowing them out, putting cannabis in them and posting them off.

Christmas
Margaret Mullins middle in front row group of children

Tenants' Party at Swythamley

2nd from left Jim Mountfort, in front of fire Ada Garrard, bottom right Pete Gratton

4th from left Beryl Gratton, next right Eric Cook, next Ken Belfield

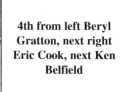

Clockwise from back left

George Riley, Ada Belfield, Lily Mountfort, Millicent Riley, Nancy Cook, Michael Goldman, Derek Riley, Philip Mountfort, Margaret Mullins, Sylvia and Doreen Mountfort with Gillian Riley between, Philip Cook

**Bryan Worsley,
Philip Mellor and
Les the landlord of
the Ship, 1960s.**

Wincle Vicarage 1948
Mrs Clowes celebrates 50 years as Sub Post-mistress at Wincle Post Office
Seated: Mrs Elliot, Rev. Elliot, Winnie Clowes, Mrs Clowes, Edna Clowes, Ellen Clowes, Mrs Goodwin
2nd row: Mrs Allen, Nellie Roberts, Millie Burnett, Mrs Brocklehurst, Bessie and Brian Gibson, Ruth Bailey,
Louis Yeates (Swythamley Hall), Millicent Riley, Phyllis Brunt, Hilda Warren, Mrs Grantham,
Mrs M. Downes, Sydney Goodwin
Some names back row: Mr Gibson, - -, - -, - -, - -, Mrs Downes, - -, - -, Nellie Hyde, Tom Jones, Ellen Taylor,
Mrs Malkin, Mrs Jones, - -, Jack Allen, Mollie Aidley, Arthur Milward (behind), Jim Davenport, Ned Bratt

Tolls Farm, John and Mary Hunt

Workers at Swythamley Hall 1930 Sam Downes 2nd from left, George Gratton 4th from left

The Feeder

Folly Mill

**British-American
Ambulance Corps vehicle
at Swythamley Hall**

The Dane Valley Story

Clifford Rathbone wrote a delightful series of articles for a Macclesfield newspaper which were published as a book in 1953 and called Dane Valley Story. He describes his travels including the legends and the people he meets along the 22 miles of the River Dane from its source on the Axe Edge moors. From Three Shires Head down to Bosley Works the river is the county boundary between Staffordshire and Cheshire.

Mr Sigley at the Mill House at Gradbach showed him the watercress beds. He said in the early days he was troubled with thieves who stole watercress in the night to sell for themselves and so on many occasions he rose in the night and went out to surprise them. He showed him the waterwheel which had a diameter of 38 feet and around it 96 water pockets, each would hold 35 gallons each which at that time made it the largest pocket wheel remaining intact in England. It was geared to turn the main shaft 2,500 times with each revolution of the water wheel.

At the height of its prosperity the mill employed around 200 people and there were cottages over the river known as Doublers Row. Mr Sigley remembered the last couple to live there. When his grandfather visited from Leek he brought them tobacco for John to chew and Martha to smoke.

Further along the valley he meets Mrs Findlow from Bearda Farm who tells him about the chapel at Danebridge. Early Methodist meetings were held at Lane Head, at Wincle Grange, at a house in Danebridge, in the upper room of the old mill and in a room at Tolls Farm known as Tolls Chamber. The chapel was erected in 1834.

She had seen many changes; the old smithy had gone and the old mill was unused. Her father had worked there when they made ingredients for shoe blacking, coal slack was brought from Rushton Station and ground at the mill then put into sacks and sent to a factory.

His journey continued to Northwich where the Dane joins the River Weaver.

Pingle Cottage

Mill Flat Meadow at Gradbach with the ruins of Doublers Row in the background, 1950s

Wincle c.1910, and below, showing Ship Inn

Christine Egerton

I was bought up at Bearda Farm, Swythamley. My grandad Findlow had died young so my mum and granny took in guests and evacuees. Visitors still came when I was little; I can remember a couple who came on a regular basis from Southport and they used to take me down to the Dane. Dad asked them not to take me as I got older as he was worried that I would go on my own which I must have done one day anyway. I was only about three years old and I believe they spent all morning searching for me. Dad went down to the Dane and found my socks and shoes on the bank. He was obviously thinking the worst but went back home and just happened to go into a hen cote in the field where there were some young chickens under a brooder and I was in there with them. I do remember being under the brooder with these chickens and being very hot.

As well as milking 22 cows my parents kept a lot of hens, perhaps 3,000 on deep litter for eggs. Wraggs from Sheffield came to pick up the crates of eggs. Day old chicks came, 1,000 at a time and as I got older I got involved with them. When the pullets were moved into bigger groups in the big sheds they didn't know how to roost so for 2 or 3 nights we had to put them up onto the perches to learn them how to roost or they would just huddle together and some would get smothered.

Another job as they got to point of lay was to what they called de-beak them. where the end of the top part of the beak was taken off. I didn't like that job but it was thought necessary to stop feather pecking. If the hens took to pecking they would actually peck another one to death. We also had to vaccinate for coccidiosis; Dad catching them, Mum would hold them and I would inject them under the wing.

The house sits on top of a steep bank above the River Dane and is very old; the stair walls are wattle and daub, and it was cold. One of the bedroom floors was uneven and Dad said on the first night when they were married they woke up the next morning and the bed had rolled down this sloping floor and jammed against the door so in all the years I was there I remember the beds sitting on hollowed out blocks of wood to stop them running away.

There was a slopstone in the old kitchen and an outside toilet a mile off down the garden. That was a two-seater earth closet where I remember sitting with mother and the waste literally fell away down the bank behind. When we built one near to the back door - an Elsan - that seemed wonderful.

The water came from a spring up at the Hannel and only trickled so water was sparse and we had to be careful with it. We had a generator - no mains electric until 1963. We were tenants of Sir Philip and Dad always spoke very well of him as being a very fair man; a very good landlord and wonderful with the older tenants. I used to go to the Hall to play with the butler's daughter, Audrey, but we had to be careful to stay in the right quarters.

I spent hours playing in the woods with Christine Bray and Malcolm Belfield; he was older and so perhaps was expected to look after us. We saw lots of deer and other wildlife. It was Sunday School every week; Mum and Sidney Gibson were the leaders for a long time. There would be in the teens of us; all the local kids went through. Mum also played the organ for the service.

Ernest Findlow with Marjorie and Grace 1920s

Ernest and Edith at Bearda

Below Danebridge Sunday school children 1957

John Egerton

In about 1966 my father-in-law, Fred Brunt had gone on holiday. He rang to say he had forgotten to pay the rent which was £120 so I went up to the Tenant's Hall on Rent Day. There were groups of other tenants stood around talking in hushed whispers then it was eventually my turn to go into the estate office up the outside stairs at the side of the Tenant's Hall. Sir Philip was behind a big desk and Mr Hall the agent stood there dressed in tweeds. They both looked surprised because I wasn't a tenant.

Sir Philip says, 'Yes Egerton, what is it?' I said, 'I've come to pay Mr Brunt's rent; he's away and it's slipped his mind.' Sir Philip replied, 'What do you mean he's forgotten his rent, that's no bladdy use!' Mr Hall muttered that it wasn't good enough so I said, 'I've just come to pay it, if you don't want it, I'll go.' I turned round and walked out. Sir Philip then shouted 'Egerton! Egerton you come back here. If you've come to pay the rent, get it paid.'

Tenants' Hall

He was dressed as usual in riding breeches and boots and while Mr Hall made the cheque out Sir Philip commented that it seemed his tenants were becoming better off than he was as they now owned cars and could take holidays. *'I think we need an increase in the rent'* But I don't know if that did happen.

The Brocklehursts of Swythamley

Swythamley Park was one of the larger estates in the upper Dane Valley. Starting as a grange of Dieulacres Abbey in the 13th century, it was granted to William Trafford of Wilmslow on the dissolution of the monasteries by Henry VIII. The family later acquired much of the adjacent land in the manor of Heaton, eventually becoming the Lords of the Manor, but at the same time running short of money. Thus in 1831 the estate had to be sold and it was bought at auction by John Brocklehurst, a prominent Macclesfield silk manufacturer from a non-conformist family.

John had three sons and a daughter Mary; sons John and Thomas ran the silk business and William managed Brocklehurst Bank, set up with his brothers. John and William married two sisters, Mary and Anne Coare, daughters of a wealthy London wine merchant. William and Anne remained childless but John and Mary more than made up for them by having eight; Philip Lancaster Brocklehurst (reputedly conceived in the town of his middle name) was their youngest son, born in 1827, but was informally adopted and reared by his Uncle and Aunt William (as they were known!).

On father John's death in 1839 William inherited Swythamley. When he died 20 years later it was his adopted son Philip Lancaster to whom he left the estate, though not without some controversy as his brothers felt unfairly treated.

Like his uncle before him, Philip expanded the estate by buying up nearby farms and countryside on both sides of the River Dane. So much so he was soon included amongst the prominent landowners (acre-ocracy) of the country. We know, for instance, his holdings went from 4134 acres in 1876 to 5320 in 1882. In 1869 he had Bagstones built in Wincle as a summer house for his sister Marianne and her friend Mary Booth. He developed Swythamley into one of the prime shooting estates of the country with many a prominent visitor coming to shoot grouse or deer; Philip himself was a good shot and noted horseman.

He had the many trees planted across the estate, including the rhododendrons[1] so ubiquitous in the area until recently, so fashionable in the 19th century[2]. It was he too who had the wire bridges strung across the Dane. He helped to improve communications with the outside world by subsidising a local post service and he improved some of the local roads; in the 1860s a bridge was built across the stream at Old Smithy in Swythamley and he part funded the building of the new Dane bridge in 1869 which still stands today. As a landowner Philip Lancaster was very much one to defend his rights with many a poacher ending up in gaol and locals having to pay tolls to travel over his land, even for funerals or to preach at Danebridge Chapel. He was known as a good, if not generous landlord for his tenants.

1. He even left £200 in his will for more to be planted in the grounds of Swythamley Hall
2. They are now being attacked by Phytophthera and are having to be removed and burnt

PLB Senior with Rathen

Philip Lancaster married late. In 1884 he got engaged to a much younger lady, Annie Lee Dewhurst, married her that same year and within four years had three children: Mabel Annie, Philip Lee and Henry Courtney.

As a prominent landowner Philip became a JP and later deputy lieutenant and sheriff for Staffordshire. In 1903 he was made a baronet in the King's Birthday Honours. However, his prime interest was always his Swythamley Estate. As the *Leek Times* wrote in his obituary in May 1904: '...in no sense could he be deemed a public man, or one interested in any affairs but his own. He lived the quiet life of a country gentleman, wedded to sport, and neither

interfering nor brooking interference.' It seems he was very canny with his money too, for he left over £300,000 to his heirs, a real fortune in those days. His widow, Lady Annie had a chapel built which was dedicated to his memory in September 1905. It was used regularly by the family and estate tenants until the 1950s. Today it is a private house.

The Swythamley Estate and the baronetcy were inherited by Philip's eldest son, Sir Philip Lee Brocklehurst. Both the younger Sir Philip and his brother received a top class education, at Bilton Preparatory School and then Eton. Philip went on to Trinity Hall, Cambridge, but did not complete his degree though he did box for the university. Perhaps of more influence on their later life was being taught to ride and

PLB Junior c.1910 and above

Swythamley Hall

Below:
The old Dane bridge, Chapmans Row in the background, only two storeys at that time

**PLB Junior and
Gwladys 1913**

**Pre World War 1
at the Hall**

**Michael Goldman outside the
Coach House**

shoot on the Swythamley Estate, and listening to the adventures of big game hunters who visited from time to time, such as Frederick Selous and John Millais.

Both boys joined the Derbyshire Yeomanry as soon as they had finished school but it was Courtney, like many younger sons, who went on to make a career in the army. He joined the 10th Royal Hussars in 1908 and served with them in India, and South Africa (lots of game hunting in those two places) and France and Flanders in WW1. Yearning for action, he soon got bored of trench warfare so he left to join the RFC in September 1916. He was posted to German East Africa and then Palestine. He returned to England mid 1918, married a very aristocratic lady, Lady Helen Mitford, daughter of the Countess of Airlie who was lady in waiting to the queen, and was sent off to northern Russia where he spent a few months in Murmansk helping to hold off the Bolsheviks. Then, instead of settling down with his new wife, he found himself a job as Game Warden of the Sudan, a post he held from 1922 till 1931. Their son, John Ogilvy, was born in 1926 but was mentally handicapped in some way and was hidden away. Helen divorced Courtney in 1931 on the grounds of adultery, he resigned his job and moved back up north and lived in Roche House.

Still in search of adventure he decided to make a name for himself, by becoming the first Brit to shoot a giant panda. He succeeded and his stuffed panda was displayed at various exhibitions in the UK and Germany in the late 1930s. You can now see it in the West Park Museum in Macclesfield. Locally he is best known for establishing a private zoo on the Roches in 1936. He was given some surplus stock from Whipsnade Zoo on condition they had a right to half the offspring. The animals included the famous wallabies, yaks, emus and various sorts of antelope. Not all the locals were specially enamoured with the new inhabitants. The yaks in particular were known to tip cars and lorries over when in the mood. During WW2 some of the animals escaped and the wallabies went on to form a breeding colony which survived at least until the early 2000s.

When WW2 broke out Courtney volunteered for action. He wasn't accepted immediately but eventually he was asked to lead a mission to southern Abyssinia where he was to get the tribes to rise up against the Italians. However, politics got in the way and he was ordered to abandon his mission. After a brief interlude in Somalia he was sent to Burma to help train the Chinese in guerrilla warfare to help them resist the Japanese invasion of their country but before he could get going properly the Japanese invaded Burma so he was put in charge of a small unit that was to hinder

Courtney mid-1920s

their advance. However his unit was forced to retreat and as they tried to make their way back to India Courtney disappeared, presumed drowned. His date of death on the Rangoon Memorial is 28 June 1942.

The young Sir Philip was lured away from Cambridge by meeting Ernest Shackleton in 1907. Philip was looking for adventure and Shackleton for funding for his expedition to Antarctica. Philip persuaded his mother to lend Shackleton a considerable sum and he was duly appointed assistant geologist, a position he had absolutely no qualification for. Philip had been hoping to accompany Shackleton on his attempt to reach the South Pole but he lost his big toe to frost bite early on, whilst climbing Mount Erebus. Instead he formed part of the South Western Party doing geological surveys and taking photos and films.

He returned in 1909 and having reached the age of maturity on Mt Erebus now had an estate to run, but that didn't preclude more adventures. He went game hunting in each of the next four years and in 1913 even whilst on honeymoon with his new bride, Gwladys Murray. In WW1 he served with the 1st Life Guards in Flanders where he was wounded in the shoulder and in 1918-9 he was in Sudan with the Anglo Egyptian Army. Military service did not stop him producing two daughters, Anne born in 1915 and Pamela in 1917.

After the war it seems the family was a little short of money. In 1920 many of the farms on the estate were put up for auction, though not all of them sold. A year later Bagstones too was offered for sale though in the end that remained in the family as Lady Annie's residence until she died in 1951.

Sir Philip re-joined his Yeomanry regiment and eventually rose to the rank of Brevet Lt Colonel. When he could, he still travelled the world with his wife Gwladys; to Egypt and Sudan to visit his brother, to New Zealand and, most adventurous of all, in 1930 they drove two small lorries from Algiers to Khartoum via northern Nigeria, crossing the Sahara on the way.

As a landowner Sir Philip was just like his father; the public had to pay to access it, a shilling to visit Lud Church, or 2/6d to climb on the Roches, though he stopped that once or twice as he found they made too much mess. In season there would be a shoot on the Roches on the Saturday and on Gun Hill on the Sunday with many prominent guests, the Duke of Devonshire being one of the most notable. As landlord he kept rents low but did little maintenance - that was left to the tenants; on the other hand he would always find a place to live for a newly married daughter or recently widowed wife of a tenant. Many locals remember fondly the Christmas parties given in the Tenant's Hall.

Sir Philip had a rather odd taste in pets. Specially remembered are his monkeys (actually baboons; he had two, the first returning with him from Sudan in 1919) and the badgers. All of these animals could be rather destructive at times.

In the Second World War Swythamley Hall was used as a convalescent hospital. Sir Philip initially became a recruitment officer and was later sent to Jordan where he used his knowledge of Arabic to help set up an Arab Legion. Lady Gwladys too did her bit - first as an ambulance driver in Coventry and then as a YMCA tea lady supporting the troops in North Africa and Italy. She was awarded an MBE for her services. Maybe the war drove them apart, for shortly afterwards they divorced.

In 1952 Sir Philip married the somewhat younger Audrey Mackenzie, who like Gwladys was a rather adventurous lady; she had been a pilot in the Air Transport Auxiliary during the War. However it seems the marriage was never really a successful one. She didn't take to life in the country and after a few years they lived separate lives, and Sir Philip was not averse to visiting Gwladys in her new home at that time. He died in January 1975. He had no male heirs and his daughters

Philip and Gwladys 1930

had no children, so the title passed to Courtneys son, John Ogilvy. However he died in 1981 and with him the baronetcy became extinct. Sir Philip left the Estate to his sister Mabel's grandson, Johnny van Haeften.[3]

With death duties as high as they were at the time, Johnny felt he had no choice but to sell it off. It went for auction in October 1977. The Hall and its parkland were bought by World Government for the Age of Enlightenment who opened it as a centre for transcendental mediation. As for the rest of the estate, in most instances the incumbent tenant was able to purchase their property if they wished. It is they, and their successors, who have turned the upper Dane valley into what it is today.

Alan and Judy Weeks

1931

Later years

3. Mabel married a Dutch Baron, Frans van Haeften in 1905

In 1874 PLB snr published a book for private circulation called *Swythamley and Its Neighbourhood* mostly written by him. Here are a few items of interest from it; the first item is from the foreword to a reprint of it published by Silk Press in 1998.

At the annual rent day in 1876 the tenants presented him (PLB) 'with a silver collar for his favourite mastiff as a thank you for the many benefits we enjoy through your praiseworthy effort in establishing a daily Post, Money Order Office and Savings Bank in this district. Many of us remember when our letters had to remain a week in the town till some farmer returning from market could bring them, probably too late to be of service.... and for the great improvement made in our public roads which at one time were so dangerous to travel.'

Two ladies have built a summer residence overlooking the valley of the Dane. The place is known by the name Bakstone for bake-stones (bak-stones) were got from a quarry in the wood behind the house. Near the Bagston Wood is a remarkably fine oak, the trunk measuring more than twenty feet in circumference.

The roads in the neighbourhood were only suitable for strongly built carts or travellers on horseback, narrow, badly kept and dangerous - the country folk and farmers (used) the old fashioned method of conveying their buxom wives and daughters on pillions behind them on horseback.

There is a deep, dark pool called Otters Pool. In 1868 a young man, a poacher had jumped from a rock but it was presumed he struck his head as he dived. A fisherman and the gamekeeper, James Barber found the body of the naked man in the pool.

A Royal of eleven tines was shot by Mr Philip Brocklehurst on Oct 7th 1869 after a severe stalk of several hours through a difficult and thickly wooded country. It was late in the evening before a shot could be obtained; the muckle harte stood with nose upraised winding his pursuers when the fatal bullet caused him to rear and fall headlong down a rocky precipice into the River Dane on the Cheshire side of Whitelee farm. He was of enormous size weighing upwards of twenty stones.

The stables (at the Hall) had accommodation for 18 horses. In the gamekeepers sanctum would be found weapons captured from poachers - six feet quarter staves inlaid with knife blades, man traps, nets, helmets and shields of wickerwork, truncheons and implements for offence and defence. The kennels were filled with setters and pointers, spaniels, terriers and mastiffs. There were workshops - a forge and boiling and steaming houses where food for the kennels and cart stables was prepared; a joiner's shop and lathe room with machinery turned by a turbine; everything done on the premises from building a wheelbarrow to a farmhouse.

**1869
The Oak. White Lee Lane**

**Early 1920s, same
car as page 74,
different use.**

**At Swythamley
Market day pre 1874
Jack Barber and Chris Dale**

Philip photographing Gwladys and Lady Annie.

Philip, Anne and a friend

Philip with his two daughters Anne and Pamela, also Courtney and his wife Lady Helen c.1920

Margaret Mullins

My grandfather, Arthur Gratton, came to work for Sir Philip as head gardener at the Hall in 1895. About the turn of the century, 1900, they were living at the newly built South Lodge and my father, George was born, the 2nd youngest of a large family. When he left school at the age of thirteen, he went to work with his father in the gardens but developed his skills to take on plumbing, electrics and car mechanics. He even went to London to attend a course at the Bentley car factory. There was a huge engine and generator in the estate yard which made the electricity for the hall; he maintained that.

In early 1930 Sir Philip and his wife Gwladys with George as mechanic made a journey from Algiers to Khartoum, crossing the Sahara in two cars. According to Lady Brocklehurst's diary they were British made Chevrolets though they were customised and with extra fuel and water tanks.

Some excerpts from Lady B's diary:

Jan 25th. Up to this year only convoys of three cars have been allowed to cross the Sahara from Algeria. Went to see the Trans-saharien people who were very discouraging. Said we should never find the track and that we were mad to go without wireless on the cars. They offered to lend us an apparatus and operator but we don't want the extra weight. Sand storms are the great danger as the track is easily obliterated and then one can only find the direction by compass.

Feb 1st. Terrible going, everything on the cars rattling and crashing and a very strong head wind blowing clouds of sand. The last 25 miles real desert, nothing but sand and very deep at that; could only run on 2nd or 3rd speed. The sand looks like clouds of smoke rolling across the ground; it gets into everything, even your mouth and behind your goggles.

Feb 4th. We have got 12 big petrol drums each holding about 10 gallons, 6 on each car and 36 gallons in the tanks which allows for nearly 1000 miles running, not too big a margin as it is 850 miles to Gao direct and one must reckon on possible divergencies and accidents. Everything has packed in very well, we have deflated our tyres till the wall is almost on the ground. This apparently is the whole secret of getting through sand successfully and (we) have given the Trans drivers three bottles of whiskey to drink our healths. Can't think of anything more to do except go to bed.

Feb 6th. Got up at 5 and started before 6, very heavy sand for 15 miles and cars boiled every few miles. Very hot although cloudy. Finished one tank of water. We were terribly thirsty and had a drink ourselves nearly every time we filled the radiators; water quite hot and dark yellow. It is 75% magnesia, so really increases one's thirst but the sand and dust make ones mouth so dry one can't resist drinking. I got stuck twice and Phil once but by shovelling away the sand with our hands and two of us pushing, we got out without using the planks. We had two cupfuls of water each to wash with. Our faces are quite orange from the sand and I don't think my nails will ever recover.

Feb 9th. We got in to Gao about 1; it is terribly hot in the middle of the day and the cars boiled a good deal. A most comfortable hotel and we immediately drank quantities of every sort of liquid and then had hot baths. I managed to stop up the waste pipe with the dust and sand that came off me in layers.

**On the road to
Laghout**

Nigeria

**Lady B and the Shell agent at
El Golea, Sahara**

Cameroon, a river to cross - and below

French Niger, the entrance to Zoria

Feb 11th. Washed the cars in the morning while George soldered a leaky joint in the petrol pipe and Phil greased the chassis. Had a very bad night, eaten alive by mosquitos and sand flies.

After more adventures travelling through Nigeria and Sudan, arriving in Khartoum Lady B sums up:

The Chevs finished their journey of 5381 miles in splendid condition. The only spare we had used was one valve spring; otherwise we never had to open the bonnets. We never changed a plug, never had the slightest trouble starting up in the mornings and the engines were always giving of their best on the entire journey. I averaged 18 miles to the gallon for the entire distance; P.s. car slightly less, 12 to 14 and we had one puncture all the way. The Chevrolet has again given a lead by being the first cars to come through from Algiers to Khartoum.

My father summed things up differently. He said, 'It was too hot, too much sand and too many flies!' He brought back a Fez and a Topee Solar which we children played with.

My father also enjoyed football and boxing. There was a huge shed known as the drying shed which had been used as a riding school and I think they had a boxing ring there too; I can remember boxing posters in

Snow ridding at West Lodge

George, Peter and Margaret

there. My father sparred with Sir Philip and recollected that one time he got confident but the next thing he knew he was waking up by the fire in the hall; Sir Philip had knocked him out!

My mother came just after the war from Liverpool. She had been in the Land Army in Wales and she came and worked with the Guernsey cattle herd that were kept on the estate farm.

Beryl (Mum) working with the Guernsey cows at Swythamley farm buildings late 1940s.

Syd Cox

I was a ten year old London evacuee. On a Sunday in early June 1940 we boarded a train to Leek then went by coach to Rudyard where the younger ones including my young brother were dropped off, then the boys and teachers were dropped off. There were 8 of us left and the headmaster said we were going to Heaton - spelt with an H not the posh Eton. We arrived at Gun End School to meet the Headmistress Miss Bratt and a reception committee in the single class room where we had tea. A local man then took 3 of us to our new homes and after a mile walk I was first to be dropped off at the South Lodge of Swythamley Park, the home of the local landowner, Sir Philip Brocklehurst. At the lodge lived Mr Arthur Gratton, and his daughter Lottie. They made me most welcome and suggested I call her Auntie and him Grandad. He was head gardener at the Hall, and was a very agile 73 years old. He had worked there since 1895 and had many tales to tell me of years gone by.

Auntie was a dressmaker and for years had lived at Sutton Hoo where she had been dressmaker to Mrs Pretty who gave the Sutton Hoo Viking ship gold treasure to the British Museum. She had tales to tell as she was a travelling companion to Mrs Pretty and had been on a trip around South Africa. Auntie came home in 1938 to tend her mother who unfortunately died.

Rushton Well
Dressing Committee
Grandad Gratton
front left

Grandad and I soon got on very well as we were both keen football fans. He was very fit for his age with a full head of hair and always wore a cap, shirt, separate collar and tie, waist-coat where he kept his pocket watch and button up cardigan with two pockets. He enjoyed smoking his pipe and was a hard worker; he was always gone by the time I got up for school. He came home for dinner and always had a half hour nap on the sofa with old Teke the dachshund curled up behind his knees. Teke went everywhere with him, even if it was only to stoke the church boiler. They would go back to the gardens till 5 o'clock. Saturdays he finished at 12.00, but in the summer he would go back again to water and close the greenhouses up. Sunday morning he would go to open them up, then back in the late after noon to water and close up. I often went with him; in war time we had double summer time, and at 5 o'clock it was too hot to close up so he had to go back after tea.

Teke

He tended the Lodge garden where he grew strawberries, raspberries, peas, potatoes and other vegetables. He also maintained the church, which included lighting the boiler every winter week-end. I would wheel the coke round for him, sometimes he let me stoke up and clean out. Once we went up into the belfry and out on to the top of the tower to look around; if we were invaded he was to ring the bells but it was not until peace was declared that they would be rung.

On the grouse shoot he was a gun loader, and he went on any fox shoot. He often shot a rabbit for the pot; he would take Teke with him into the church grounds and when she got on the scent of a rabbit she started yelping and drove it round to grandad. Bang! There was our dinner. He loved his shooting and was a good shot.

As a lad he was ice skating on the canal with a clay pipe in his mouth; he fell over and bit the pipe right in half. He saw Blondin, a famous French tight rope walker walk across Rudyard Lake; he was famous for walking across Niagara Falls.

At the lodge there was a Pears Soap Cyclopedia; anything I wanted to know Auntie would say 'Look it up in Pears'. Inside was a copy of a famous painting, Bubbles by John Millais, who was a friend of old Sir Philip and some times visited the hall. When grandad started work for old Sir Philip there were 6 or 8 men under him and he was not expected to work, just delegate. But by 1940 it was him and Bob Heath, and Tom Hill as a labourer.

The milk lorry dropped the papers at the lodge; we had the *Daily Express*, then Michael would come to pick up the rest and deliver them. I liked going into the potting shed, because there was a carpenter's tool chest full of tools; grandad once made a wheel-barrow. There were tools for making cartridges, and casting lead shot, all from a bygone era; a schoolboy's delight. He loved showing people round his gardens, I was with him when he showed round some of the new Red Cross staff when they came to the Hall. Mrs White was the matron; Olive Wilshaw worked there with Edna Poyser. Once a week Michael would take him to Macc to sell any surplus produce to a Mrs Mottishead who had a greengrocers shop, otherwise he seldom went far. He was also the M.C. when there were whist drives or dances in the Tenant's Hall.

They told me a tale of Tom Whittaker, Olive's grand-father, He would go for a drink at the Ship Inn, coming home past the lodge he would be saying 'Lost, where am I?' and many a night grandad got his torch to see him over the bridge. One night he was saying lost and an owl hooted 'whoo'... He replied. 'Tom Whittaker'.

Near to South Lodge was Hilly Lees Farm where Mr and Mrs Harold Hine lived and Joe Findlow worked there. After tea Joe would come past the lodge on his bike to fetch the cows up from Crabtree field for milking and to feed two lots of hens. I would quickly run to catch up with Joe, and his dog Floss. Joe was about 16, and I got on very well with him, my main aim was to ride his bike as I had never ridden a bike before.

Swythamley School 1924

**Heaton Lowe
1930s**

**Swythamley
Church**

Swythamley School 1922

Swythamley School 1926

Brassington family, Hollin Hall

Joe let me ride and held on to the bike till one day he let me go, I only stopped when I ran into the back of the cows, after that I could go solo.

Harold had a milking machine which few other farmers around there had at that time; the only other was Jim Findlow at Buxton Brow, who also generated his own electricity. I followed Joe when ploughing; he had a two horse, two furrow plough with extra blades at right angles, so at the end, he tipped it up and went straight back again. Most farms still had single furrow ploughs

Swythamley Home Guard Platoon was formed around 1941. They were kitted out with full army uniforms, including forage cap, gaiters, boots and rifles. Their shoulder flashes were Home Guard; I think 5th North Staffs. Ken Turner the estate agent was the officer, the sergeant was Bill Semple, the gamekeeper from the Roches; the corporal was Louis the butler from the Hall. The rest of the platoon that I remember were George Gratton, old Pev Poyser who I think was the oldest one, son Douglas, Herbert Cooke, Jack Belfield, Joey Aidley, Clarry Findlow from Buxton Brow, George Riley, Frank Pool

Hannel Farm, Swythamley

from Gun End, Joe Gould, George Kirkham, Stan Millward, Matthew Berrisford, Herbert Findlow and Bailey from Hanging Stone.

They would parade every Thursday evening in the Tenant's Hall. Instructors would visit to teach weapon training and rifle shooting; they had to go to Leek to fire on the rifle range and also to go on manoeuvres. A .22 rifle team was formed and they used the Tenant's Hall for their matches.

I had a year in the single class room at Gun End School under Miss Bratt; she was a very good teacher and taught us to knit for the armed forces and read stories from *Jungle Book*. The winter of '40-41 was severe and we had about 6 weeks off school. In Sept 1941 I went to Leek County Secondary school by bus. I left school at Easter 1944 and there was talk of finding me a job on the estate, but my London grandfather had arranged for me to be an apprentice carpenter at his firm. So with a heavy heart I went back to London. I went home once in 1942 for 2 weeks and my mother visited me each summer for a week. I had spent 4 very happy and wonderful years of freedom and doing things like ferreting, grouse beating, hay making, corn-stooking, potato and turnip picking, and all sorts of jobs and things I would have missed had I stayed in London.

Wartime at Swythamley Hall. Millicent Riley 4th from right third row.

Joyce Matthews

My husband, Brian and I went to live in a flat at Parkhouse, Swythamley in 1967. I was the housekeeper to Dorothy Knight who lived there as a tenant on the Swythamley Estate. Sir Philip and Dorothy at that time were long time companions and would sometimes ride together; he on his horse Solly and Dorothy on her horse. He came nearly every night for his evening meal until he died. He used to drive up for a while and then one of us used to fetch him

PLB

Swythamley Park

up the track. I thought it was very creepy if I had to go. He was living in the hall on his own at that time with his Pekinese dog, Silver. It was dark with no lights or only dim ones. Dorothy had the meal ready in the dining room - she did everything properly and then they moved into the library to the fire and later she ran him back.

I found him to be a nice kind man; he lent me a car at one time for 9 months. He used to have 3 Mini Clubman estate cars and he said 'Go anywhere you like in the park'. Jim Mountfort was the stockman and they kept belted Galloways but he also milked two Jersey cows and I went down through the green gates every day to fetch a quart of Jersey milk. There were stalls for 16 cows and a bull pen at the small dairy. We were allowed to go anywhere and when the estate was sold and the Meditation people came they were also good to get on with but when Mr Naylor bought it all that stopped; he wanted it all to himself. It had been a wonderful life and a privilege to know Sir Philip.

An event that stands out in my memory is the flash flood of June 1989 which caused tremendous damage in the Wildboarclough area. I was at Tolls farm in Danebridge where I kept my horse with Fay Wood. We were about to get the horses in when we heard an almighty roar and a tidal wave of water came crashing down the Dane which flooded into the football field by the bridge. The horses panicked, jumped out of the field and galloped up towards the Ship. The surge of water quickly subsided and the field was left with lots of fish flapping about so a group of us ran round trying to rescue them and put them back in the river.

Geoff Allen

My mother, Grace Findlow came from Bearda Farm and my dad, Jack Allen from Coppice Side, Heaton. My Grandad Findlow farmed Bearda Farm which was on the Swythamley Estate but he died young. When they wanted to get married dad put in for the job of Water Bailiff and they went to live at Feeder Cottage in 1934. His job was to maintain the Feeder and keep the water levels right. It is a remarkable piece of engineering being level so that water from the River Dane can feed Rudyard Lake and also run back into the Dane should it be necessary. And of course it would all have been dug by hand when it was constructed.

He walked the length of the feeder every day down to the lake and then walked round checking if the fishermen had got a licence and if not he could issue a day licence. He had to keep the canal clear which involved mowing it out with a scythe and also mowing the sides. He made hay of the stretch from Feeder Cottage to Thompson Bridge and there were two little fields as well. He kept half a dozen cattle, a pig and some hens. He would milk an odd one or two for our own use; mother did teas. Trains from Manchester and the other way brought visitors to Rushton and they walked up the Feeder path and then up the Dane to Danebridge and back when they would stop for a cup of tea and a scone. It could be very busy at weekends.

When it had rained hard dad had to go and measure what water was coming off the Dane into the canal and if it was over full at Rudyard he had to open the paddles along the feeder and let it back to the river. One night it had rained hard and he got up in the middle of the night and on his way back he fell into the Dane which was in flood. Luckily he fell into a side pool so he could get his-self out again - he couldn't swim.

The fish ladders and weirs were in good order then and I remember in the season watching fish jumping up them. Below Gig Hall Bridge on a hot summer day people would come and dive into the basin there. There were plenty of fish in the feeder too; roach, perch and pike. My cousins came up at weekends and we would catch them. Mostly we threw them back but once we caught 104 and kept them all and my uncle cut them up and we ate what we could. We had corn and stuff left at Thompson Bridge and we fetched that with a punt or the pony and cart.

We used to go playing on the Flats, the flat fields over the river belonging to Whitelee. I learned to ride my pushbike there. We used to go up to Whitelee and help with the haymaking and go into the woods watching foxes and badgers playing. We went to Barleyford Woods for blackberries and spent a lot of time in the Dane where we caught Bullnobs and later let them go again. We were always in water but we never could swim.

In wartime I think there was an army deserter holed up at Gig Hall for a while. I guess he helped them until either he was found or gave himself up.

We moved to Rushton in 1949 and dad became a postman. His father had done it before and had given up in 1946. He did all round Wincle and up to Back Forest. The round was 18 mile, all on foot. He called at Danebridge Post Office on the way back to pick the mail up and then worked his way back emptying the mail boxes to drop off at Rushton where it was picked up. He started at 6am and got back at between 3 and 4 pm.

It is so sad to see the canal these days; it is a disgrace when you think of all the hard work that went in over all those years.

**The fish ladders on the
Dane c.1908**

Gig Hall

Jack at Goldenhill
1947

Jack Allen
presented with
retirement
certificate at
Rushton Post
Office

GIG HALL, DANE VALLEY.

**Mr Pev Poyser at
Swythamley**

Jean Higginson

My grandad, Pevril Poyser was a tenant at Pool Farm, Swythamley and when Sir Philip had to sell a few farms he bought the Old Smithies. He farmed at Swythamley for 40 years and was well known for poaching so he wasn't popular with Sir Philip. During the First War he used to kill horses for the Black Market; he could dress anything and would hang the meat in tripods of hay and then sell it to people in Manchester. He was well known in horse dealing circles.

We used to play in the woods at the Old Smithies; in the second world war they cut two woods down and took the timber for the war effort - one at the back and down in front of the house. They wanted the wood and just came and took it. They were supposed to replace it after the war but it's all ferns now.

**Early 1930s, Pev on the load with visitors
from Manchester**

Alan Blackhurst

My family bought the 180 acre farm at Barleigh Ford (Barleyford) in 1967 from Eric Bailey. I moved with my mum and dad and my granny, Mary Blackhurst on November the 5th. The awful foot and mouth epidemic had started and so we were hardly able to move from the place after that. Fortunately we hadn't a lot of stock to start with but everyone had to take their milk churns to the end of the road near to Rushton. When things settled down later we built a milk stand at the end of Eardleys road and took our churns there every day. We carted 20 churns, ten at a time in the back of the Landrover. They were picked up by Weavers but later on George Mitchell from Bosley picked them up and he came into the yard for them.

The farmhouse is very old and built of brick; there is a stone above a fireplace in a bedroom with the date 1565 carved on it. We were told that the clay to make the bricks was cut out from a field near to Whitelee which was called Marl Meadow. There were also boundary stones around the farm; I knew of at least 3 or 4. They were like small stone gate stumps with WMS carved on them for William Matthew Stow. The house was covered in ivy when we went there but we cut a lot of it down as it was too big.

There had been a lot of felling in the woods in wartime; we were told that there was a big copper beech tree near to the yard and Mrs Oliver who lived there then wouldn't let them have it. There were a lot of deer and pheasants and a friend of the family, Ken Mitting, who was a surgeon, sometimes shot deer. Through this we once had Blaster Bates shooting. Also with Peter Moody from Nantwich an American called Sam Saxton. He owned graveyards all over the world where Americans were buried. He shot a stag and sent us a wonderful letter.

......I can't tell you how much I appreciate your hospitality and the experiences we shared together in your kitchen and in the barn and bringing the Great Stag back to the house.....

The great horns were shipped as my personal baggage from Manchester to London, London to Philadelphia. Everybody remarked about them. They ended up in Clearfield along with the skin on a dark, snowy, cold, wind-blown night when I dropped them off at a little airport in this more desolate area of Pennsylvania where the Clearfield Taxidermy exists.....

My mouth still waters when I think of your home-cured bacon. My ears can still hear Granny talking as she sits beside the fire.....

Samuel B Saxton

Barley Ford

Barley Ford

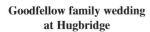

**Mr and Mrs
Blackhurst and
Alan**

Wall Hill

**Goodfellow family wedding
at Hugbridge**

Anson Franklin

I was born here at Higher Minn End in 1932; our folks have been here since 1929. It was rented then from Mr Mason. My grandparents lived at 7, Bosley Works and dad (Anson) was born there. Grandad, Walter Franklin, had served his time at Pool End near Leek as a blacksmith then he used to travel and shoe tram horses at Newton Heath when Manchester had horse drawn trams. My great grandad, Anson, helped to lay the Canadian Pacific Railway and drove the first steam roller that they had in Macclesfield.

We milked and kept some sheep and always had horses. Donkeys years ago dad bought a half-legged one with a flaxen mane and tail. She was running loose in a little wood at Gun End; nobody could do anything with her. It was just before he got married then he got the offer of a good job on the railway which meant selling the horse and mother said, 'If you sell the horse, I'm not marrying you.' So they kept the horse and we've had horses ever since. Mother loved horses; she came from Wood Cottage, Wincle and Grandfather Bullock kept Shires - they had the Wincle prefix going back to when the Shire Horse Society started in the 1870s.

We were the second farm around here to have a milking machine in the 1930s; Mr Fallows from down near the chapel was the first. The petrol for the little engine was not so dear then. The churns were picked up by Coopers and the milk went to Lancashire Hygienic Dairies or Beswick's Co-op or the Co-op at Congleton. Before that dad used to take it to the station in 18 gallon churns - two miles down the hill to catch the half past seven milk train in the morning with a strong, light horse known as a vanner. The train used to drop cans off as it went down to Uttoxeter then as it came back, it picked the milk up for Manchester. If the train was in and the gates shut and somebody was late, the other farmers would hold the train up by leaving a churn of milk between the trucks all the time as they unloaded at one side of the gate and swapped the cans across the rails.

Dad used to supply Hammonds butchers on Moss Rose with pigs, so many every week. Mr Massey from Swallowdale used to come and kill them and then dad took them with the horse and float wrapped in clean hessian. If he was late, the old ladies used play hell; they were waiting for the liver and stuff. It was straight from slaughter, hung and to frying pan - no fridges.

I remember the road lengthsman very well; what we call Whittakers Corner, he used to leave his handcart there. Dad could remember the main road before it was tarmaced; he used to say there used to be stone brought there and they had a little box about a yard square and men would sit and nobble stone and fill this box and they got so much money per cubic yard and that was ready to mend the road.

I've heard it said my dad left Bosley School when he was 12 and he played wag the last half day to lead one of the horses in the binder cutting the corn. I was the last lad to leave the school at 14 because I was too old to move to Macc or Congleton. We walked to school and sometimes got a bus back from the Queens to the bottom of the road which cost a penny. The road was called Masons Lane then but is now Minn End Lane. You could walk the main road then and not see much traffic; you went in your clogs.

My favourite thing was nature walks and geography - the rest of it I had no interest in. I once had cane for putting caps under the desk lid and it went off BANG. It's in the punishment book; letting gunpowder off in school. It was strict; one old teacher, she was a great old lady but if she lost her temper she threw the blackboard cleaner at you and 9 times out of 10 she missed and it hit somebody else.

We spent many a happy hour in the woods listening to the birds and you could walk round the feeder up from what we call Bonds with a jam jar and fishing net for jack sharps. There used to be a place where there was a little holding pen in Cartlidge Wood where we took sheep down to the river to be washed before we sheared because the wool was worth more. It was in the Dane half way between where Shell Brook joins it and the boundary with Goodfellows. When I was a kid dad kept between 30 and 40 ewes and we all went - dad, all of us and anybody as would help. I can see now where dad and somebody else would be stood in the river washing the sheep.

There was a big pond in the river below Shell Brook where scouts from Macc would come swimming at weekends, something I never tried. I've seen the Dane in flood taking trees down. There was a bad thunderstorm further up once; we were haymaking down the bottom fields and could hear it coming. I think there were a couple of blokes lower down fishing and they got drowned.

One Sunday morning an aeroplane like a Tiger Moth came over doing stunts and that. I was getting grumbled at; we were supposed to be going down to grandad's for dinner. I came running in - it had crashed at Barleyford. Off we ran down through Cartlidge Wood. I said it was in the wood - it had disappeared into the trees. I followed dad down and the ambulance had got there. I remember the engine had broken away and was down on Barleyford Lane. We didn't get down to grandad's!

In wartime there was a searchlight battery down the road at Minn End. The first year in the snow they were in Bell Tents and used to have to wash in the feeder in cold water. Eventually they put some huts up and a cookhouse. There were three searchlights - a 14 miler and two 7s, two or three light guns and one or two lanterns across the fields to draw fire. We were under the flight path to Manchester and Liverpool so there was blackout. It was a bit frightening when the bombers went over. If it was clear you saw the barrage balloons go up at the railway works and Rolls Royce at Crewe. One broke loose one day and came sailing over here. We saw different planes picked up in the lights and handed over to another searchlight and then probably shot down. I remember once a big flare being dropped; it lit all the sky up and you could see better than with electric light. You could also see the glow of fires in Liverpool and Manchester.

They bombed Bosley you know. Lord Haw Haw married a woman from Wilmslow and one night they were on the radio. They were going to get Dane Mill at Bosley, they knew they was on war work, and the aqueduct where the canal goes over the Dane and the viaduct where the railway goes over the valley. So one night they came but started too soon and dropped the bombs too far to the west before the incendiaries. If it had been done properly everything would have been gone. When they had dropped the incendiaries it was so bright you could see the telephone wires on the main road from this yard. There was a landmine dropped at Lower House near the Harrington Arms that killed some cows. One night they dive bombed the searchlights and missed them. The bombs landed in the valley, the trees split to pieces.

A sentry box guarded as you came up the road. One Eastertime there was some nice pussy willow on a bush down there and as kids we had get some to bring a bit home. We got up by the cookhouse and I know we swapped it for some nice fruit cake. They weren't allowed pick it, but because we'd picked it they could have it and one or two were going home for the weekend and wanted take some.

Dad used get swill from there for the pigs. He used go down with horse and float and they used say, 'Be careful how you empty such a bin and you found a big chunk of fish wrapped in cabbage leaves'. So we rinsed it off and it was alright.

Evans and Bellhouse had wood stacked at Rushton during wartime out of the way of bombing and Sentinel steam wagons used shift it back and to from the docks and as they wanted it for milling. They used to get a pipe over the big feeder bridge near Chaff Hall as goes to the canal from the reservoir to fill their tanks with water for the steam. Another place was the canal at Fools Nook.

When I was a kid in the late 1930s there were 200 oaks taken out of Cartlidge Wood for building railway wagons; that was fetched out with horses. Dad bought the farm in 1948 and the wood was sold separate with a right of road through the yard to get the timber off. They went down the middle of one field and then wanted to go down the meadows but dad blew his top. Somebody from the Ministry came and said they had to pick a place and put a proper track in and when they'd finished it had to be taken up. They bulldozed tracks round the wood but we had that much trouble with them through the yard. If there was more than one wagon to be loaded, it got stuck in the yard and you couldn't have cows out or nothing; it was one lot of trouble after another. The chap had many extensions to his felling license. Most was nice big oaks - all gone but the bluebells have survived.

At the end dad got wind that a London firm were interested in buying the land so he approached the timber firm and said, 'You owe me so much money and you've got to take that track up - that's going to cost you to put it right so I'll give you so much and we'll scrub the debts. And that's how we got the wood.

I remember before we had baled hay there was a gypsy caravan used to come and park near the end of our lane. He used to come and buy a bit of hay off dad for his horses; cut a truss with the hay knife and stick a peg through it to carry it back.

I also remember the cabbage patch stag. He used to come regular for a feed in the cabbage field when I was a kid. He had a good set of antlers and used to wander off back towards Swythamley. Sometimes he'd get into the kitchen garden as well and eat the lettuce; mum used shout about it.

Dumkins was a little farm; Sammy Beardmore and Emmy were the last to live there. He used to grow some good green crop and garden stuff. You went up a ladder like going up a loft to go to bed. A lot of it was black and white and the main structure was the remains of four tree trunks; it had been built around them. There was a tiled floor and it was cobbled around where the trees were. It was unique and no electric or water and they reared 4 children there. Sammy had his corn off John Cook and I think that was the only vehicle - an old single wheel Austin wagon - that used to go up that track from Barleyford to Dumkins.

At the end of our lane and at the top of our meadow we know it as Hillgate and Lockgate. There were two gates about 20 yards apart. Lockgate was a parish boundary and the two farms up at Hawkslee had to pay a fee to the landlord of this place. One used to pay and he had a key; the other wouldn't and he had to go up the old road and come back down to Hawkslee. After a lot of trouble over the years the council agreed to take over the road and the farms above had to agree that the old road to the top was shut and only used as a footpath.

Dad used to do a lot of breaking horses in for folk like the Co-op and the railway; he'd buy and sell and they'd trade with him. Horse sales! I've walked horses from here to Leek and back again. There'd be a 100 or more of one sort or another all in their different pens and sheds; it was quite a day. He broke mainly shire and shire cross for the docks at Liverpool and Manchester. They cost £40-50.

When I was 13 in the summer before I left school I did all the mowing before I went school with a pair of horses. And harrowing, rolling, muck carting - all loaded by hand and dragged out into rucks and spread by hand. When the weather was bad you had a hessian bag over your shoulders and one round you. The fastener would be a five inch nail threaded on a twist and stuck through.

Dad used to go to Leek Market with owd Betty. One day she held the traffic up when they had put the roundabout in. They were in the habit of turning up Ashbourne Road and stabling up at the Talbot. The copper stopped him and said, You've got to go round. But she wouldn't go left; traffic was getting bunged up down Haywood Street. In the end dad dropped the reins and told the copper to take her round his self but she wouldn't go and they had to let her nip straight up Ashbourne Road.

Leek Show 1971, Dad

I remember taking calves to market in a sack. Even after we had the motor, you'd take the back seat out and put a couple in face to face.

Until I was twenty all the farm work was with horses. Dad wouldn't have a tractor; everyone used say we were crackers. He did in the end though, a little Fergy; he always said it would have to be a diesel and not a stinking TVO. Diesel was £2 for a 40 gallon drum delivered.

Our shires were first registered in 1936 and it's said that our stud - Bosley Minns - is one of the oldest still going. We kept 4 breeding mares and some younger stock. Dad loved his showing; he used to go to Altrincham, Poynton, Rochdale, Bury, Bakewell, Ashbourne, Leek, Derby, Moorgreen. We took 9 to one show and came back with 4 or 5 cups. Since dad died I think one of my proudest moments was when one of our horses was exported to America and she finished up Champion of all America. That to me was better than winning the Horse of the Year show because I'd bred her. About 6 years ago another that we'd bred stood reserve champion in Germany. You

Freda, Betty the horse and Anson

can find our breeding in Canada, Holland, France and Belgium as well.

Ellen Bailey

In the 1947 winter at Higher Minn End I was 9 years old. For 14 weeks the milk had to be taken down to the main road, across the fields with the horse and sledge, down past Venables then across the fields again to the road. The snow was 15-17 feet deep in the lane to the farm and we were shovelling it out for weeks. There was dad in the bottom shovelling up to Anson and Ernie Beard who worked for dad and then Freda and me on the top with a fire shovel to throw it over the hedge. But I never stopped off school because the teacher, Miss Roberts lived in the school house.

I did quite a lot on the farm looking eggs and feeding hens when I got home from school and at weekends cleaning them out. There was one hencote here and one there, and four down the Pit Field. I was led to believe that the bricks that the farmhouse is built from came from the marl pit there.

In wartime when the soldiers came, some would come up for supper; mum would do egg and chips and they would have a game of cards after. When they were cleaning the searchlights they could play them on the pictures in the living room, they made patterns and mum would know how many were coming up. Stan Dinsdale was a regular and asked if his wife and children from Liverpool could come up and stay away from the bombing so they came for about 3 months and to this day I keep in contact with them.

When they felled the trees in Cartlidge Wood, as the roots died down the land started slipping in places into the feeder and they had to box it because the banking wouldn't hold it. Even in the late 60s at Venables end of the feeder there was still plenty of water and full of jack sharps (sticklebacks) though its all dried up now.

Down in the wood there is a big hole full of bluey black water which we call a breathing hole. Dad put a cart rope down it with a stone on the end and it never hit the bottom; I think that was 80 feet. It's a dangerous place.

Above the feeder there are shale banks and if you break it up there are fossil shells in it. (*Perhaps that is where Shell Brook gets its name. SH*) There are stone bridges over the feeder and lots of adders. One year when it was hot our Alsatian was bitten and we had numerous sheep and sometimes cattle or horses bitten. When they were lain down if they moved at a certain moment they would be bitten usually near the throat and all swell up badly.

Ellen with Sambo

At the top of our land is a walled enclosure with 21 sycamore trees in. It was always a good shelter for young cattle and sheep and was said to be a landmark for ships coming in at Liverpool.

We had a big youth club in the schoolroom at Bosley on Monday nights. To get the young ones to come they asked the vicar, Mr Wilkinson to come and join us. He said, 'Right, on condition that you lot come and fill the back pews in church and I'll go across to the Queens with you and have a drink and a cigarette. We got membership up to 65 in the 1950s and it went until the 90s. We had darts, table tennis, music, cards, dancing to records and a Christmas party. A cup of tea or pop and biscuits after. Everybody looked forward to it.

Ellen with Betty, Queenie and Prince at Macclesfield Show 1964

Sam Hadfield

I was born on 24th February 1924 at Keepers Cottage, Bosley Brooks in the bedroom I now sleep in. It was 2am with a blizzard blowing and Nurse Lawton the village midwife walked over the Hollins Hill from the nurses cottage opposite Bullgate Lane to deliver me.

Samuel Earlam Mason going to school 1905-6,

My name was already chosen, with no options, by my Grandmother Mason of Minn End Farm. She never saw over the loss of her only son Sam, my mother's brother, who at the age of thirteen whilst taking the milk by pony and trap to Bosley station was to have an accident that he died from. The pony shied on seeing a bag blowing in the hedge, bolted and Sam was thrown out of the trap. His leg had to be amputated at home resulting in it going septic and causing his death. Sam always went to school at Bosley on his donkey and tethered it until returning home.

In the Bosley Brooks area were Hadfields, Scofields and Somerfields living at The Brooks, Brook Cottage and Brooks Farm. The postman was always getting mixed up so mother called our place Keepers Cottage. Dad was the gamekeeper for a syndicate of people - solicitors and mill owners - who must have bought the shooting rights from Lord Harrington of an area from Fools Nook over the Minns to the Dane.

William Hadfield and his daughter Miriam Rathbone and baby Pat 1940

We had no electricity; lighting was by paraffin lamp, storm lamp or candles making reading at night difficult. We had a well in the orchard and pumped water by hand for household needs but we did have a bathroom which was unusual in those days. The water supply came from a spring which never froze no matter how severe the frost was. Hot water was from a side boiler in a large cast iron kitchen range.

Our radio had to have two batteries - a large dry battery and a wet accumulator in a glass container - with a carrying handle which had to be taken to the Ice Factory in Smithy Lane to be charged by their water driven electric generator which was still in full working order when I bought the Ice factory in 1953.

I went to Bosley School at the age of five.

On my first day the older boys decided to tease me by making a ring around me and singing 'Sam, Sam the dirty man, washed his face in a frying pan, combed his hair with a donkey's tail and scratched his belly with his big toe nail.' I thought this was very funny and joined in the laughter which went down

Sam's aunt, Frances Mason from Minn End

like a lead balloon so I had no further trouble.

Mr and Mrs Mather were the teachers; when they retired they built Dane Cliff in Bennetts Lane. The new teachers were Mrs Lomax at the School House and Mrs Lindop who travelled daily from Hanley to Bosley Station and walked up the church path to school.

At Bosley Brooks, Mary Hadfield?

Two of my recollections are of the very hot summers when the tar used to melt on the roads and the very cold winters with high snowdrifts and teams of men digging the main roads out by hand before the days of salt and diggers.

At the age of ten I had a terrible scalding accident by reaching to get something from our kitchen grate mantelpiece. I fell and tipped a large black kettle of boiling water over me. This kettle boiled for 12 hours a day as a constant supply of hot water. I ended up in a wheelchair and did not attend school for over 6 months but during the time off I passed an exam to go to Macclesfield so I never went back to Bosley.

Much of the time at Macclesfield I cycled to school except in snow when myself and Ken Naden

Kathleen Hadfield modelling a family heirloom, an original shepherd's smock

Hadfield family at Bosley Reservoir

Sam

**Pat and Isobel
Rathbone**

Hadfields

Cousins from Swallowdale

from Dawsons Farm had a lift with George Mitchell in his milk lorry from Marsh Head. Another mate was Tom Wood of Top Lock, North Rode, and we spent a lot of free time rabbiting and fishing, like trying to catch the biggest pike in Bosley Reservoir where there were also plentiful perch and tickling trout in the brooks which was our speciality. We had regular customers particularly later in wartime when food was rationed. The fishing rights belonged to Yates Wine Lodge as did the land around the reservoir and the Harrington Arms was also owned by them. They gave me a permit so that I could supply them with fish so I used to supply them with big pike which they used to make pike cutlets of. There were a lot of pike in the reservoir and they made very entertaining fishing, putting up a very good fight. The tenant at the Harrington was Jimmy Haworth and there was also a slaughterhouse for the stock kept on the Harrington Ground. Yates had an advert in Blackpool and around for Bosley Beef.

There was much more wildlife in Bosley when I was a boy; the lovely call of peewits and curlews were common, also corncrake, skylarks and owls at night. Predators were strictly controlled and ground nesting birds reaped the benefit. There was what we called Peewits Field and I used to have orders from the hospital in Macclesfield for peewits eggs for some ill people. I used to take one or two out of a nest before the bird sat and she would lay again.

We had a game called lassooing tramps. There was a tip by the side of the road between the Harrington Arms and Blakefield - no dustmen then - and there were a lot of bike tyres on it. Tramps stopped at Rosedale at my grandmas - they had a sign where they knew they could get something to eat or drink. When we were coming home from school we'd go and hide behind this big hedge, get a bike tyre with a rope tied to it and as a tramp came along, drop it over his head, pull it tight and fasten it to a bush.

As my father was the local gamekeeper I spent a lot of time helping to rear the pheasants, partridge and ducks. We also had an underkeeper helping us; poaching was a great nuisance and we had alarm guns situated around the woods.

We had a gundog training school; dogs came from all over the country to North Rode Station where I used to go and collect them. They had muzzles on for travelling or they wouldn't have them in the Guards Van. My father trained them to retrieve from land or water; bringing the bird back without biting it - soft-mouthed - to drop it at the feet of the shooter. There were setters, black Labradors, pointers, a lot of spaniels - springers and cockers. We had a lot of kennels here where we kept them and they were taken out daily and when father thought they were ready they were sent back and he was paid.

There was a fair lot of heather up here then; I shot my first grouse up on the Minns. On shooting days we would start about 10.30 and try and get back for lunch. Mother used to have a hotpot boiling for the shooters in the cooking range. My job was to clean the guns and put them away in the cases at the end of the shoot and before they went home. Another lousy job was gutting all the rabbits; I've done as many as 50 in a day. I sold them to a firm called Plants in Chestergate, Macclesfield. There was a time when I could get more for the rabbit skin than I could get for the rabbit in the mid 1930s. The skins went to Stockport for hat making.

Bosley was a self contained village; we had a village policeman, PC Fox who was killed when coming down the Dumbers on his new bike with a new hub brake system which proved to be unsafe and was discontinued. The brakes failed and he was thrown off and died as a result.

There was a vicar living in the vicarage, a post office and postmen, a sweet shop kept by Mrs Smith situated on what was the village green. There were two petrol stations; one with a shop. Two haulage contractors and farm milk collectors. A coal merchant also selling paraffin. A builder, a plumber, a joiner and undertaker. A village nurse and midwife. A gamekeeper, a river bailiff and a man who lived at Swallowdale Lodge which is now demolished who maintained the feeder, brook and reservoir. There were two village lengthsmen who did a very good job of keeping the village tidy. There was a mole catcher who also cured and made up the skins. There was a blacksmith, a wheelwright, a village dressmaker, a cheesemaker and a sheepshearer. The station with stationmaster, signalmen, and track maintenance men. Two cafe and tearooms, an AA box with direct breakdown phone. Three stone quarries, Stoneyfold, Dawsons and

Swallowdale. We used to go up Swallowdale regularly because it belonged to Aunt Dorothy who owned the quarry too which a firm called Pointons from Congleton worked. The farm was tenanted by Bill Massey.

There was a threshing contractor often followed by the village rat catcher (me) with my little fox terrier, Daisy. She was the queen of ratcatchers, up to 50 on a good day and

Swallowdale Quarry

with battle scars on her face to prove it. I used to take her on my bike or motorbike in a bag on my back; she weighed 16 lbs.

In 1939 the war started and everything changed. There was strict blackout, petrol, oil, food and clothes rationing. There was strict discipline and total patriotism or internment. There was government direction as to where you worked; it must be of national importance, either agriculture, munitions, coal mining or of course the armed forces.

The two mills in Bosley worked 24 hours a day during the war; Wood Treatment Products were used in the aircraft industry and in many other uses. Bosley Pure Ice supplied ice to May and Baker who made M+B Tablets to control malaria in the armed forces serving in the Far East and Africa. May and Baker had been evacuated from Dagenham to Leekbrook to a factory belonging to Joshua Wardle for safety as they were providing a very essential service to the war effort.

There was a Home Guard unit, fully armed; I had a Sten Gun which I took home with me. My guard rota was in a hut on the Stoneyfold, 2 hours on and 2 hours off, throughout the night. There was a fire station at the Queens Arms garage and steel wire ropes across the reservoir to prevent amphibious landings in case of invasion. There are two surviving concrete pill boxes; one overlooking the reservoir and one near the canal on the Congleton Road, and there was a searchlight Army Unit in a field at Minn End Farm.

We had two Special Police Constables resident in the village and I had the honour as far as I know of being the only one copped in the village for testing a motorbike I had repaired up the Dumbers which was untaxed. I had to appear in court but was allowed to keep my driving license as I was doing my apprenticeship at Tom Simisters, the main Rover and Ford Agents in Macclesfield. After that the two Special PCs regular supply of unrationed meat (black market) in the form of rabbits, pheasants etc came to an abrupt end - the supplier went sour on them.

I went to serve in India in the Royal Engineers; we were constructing and equipping airfields for the relief of Burma and for the attack on Japan; however on the 6th August 1945 the atom bomb was dropped on Hiroshima and 3 days later on Nagasaki which resulted in the surrender of the Japanese so the airfields were no longer needed.

I had a bearer, a local Indian lad who made my bed and cleaned up and washed up and polished my brasses; it was like having a maid. He was paid one penny a week which was wealthy for them.

Communications were very poor so they asked for a despatch rider and foolishly I volunteered. My journey during the day was 300 miles and going through the villages they used to throw stones at me. The roads were dirt with sections of concrete so you could be thrown off your bike. It was a hell of a job with lots of punctures.

Whilst in India I installed the refrigeration plant on the airfields; I had no idea that a few years later I would buy Bosley Pure Ice and cold storage factory and export the whole of the machinery to Basra, Iraq in 1954.

James Earlam, my great uncle was the village blacksmith at The Smithy in Smithy Lane. He was also an inventor of farm machinery and one of his inventions was one of the first potato pickers which I believe was later manufactured by Bamfords. On being demobbed in 1947 I renovated the smithy which had been due for demolition and converted it into a workshop and later a showroom.

I bought the ice factory which was originally a good example of an old Cheshire Corn Mill. There was a big tank of brine and inside that were vats the size of big blocks of ice containing pure water which froze as the brine was reduced to a low temperature. These were then lifted out with a crane and put on tilting gear and tilted over so that the block of ice slid out and was loaded onto a wagon. Sometimes we would crush it but usually it was sold in blocks; a wagon load went every day to May and Baker. It also went to fishmongers and to hotels in Buxton. Jim Nicklin was the factory manager and lived in the house there. He also drove the truck that delivered the ice. The factory ran 24 hours a day and an old boy called Charlie Tatton worked nights. He used to hide his wage packets; they found them after he'd died all over the place up in the eaves - he'd never spent anything. It was a three storey mill and Jim Nicklin used to dry tobacco up in the top which he grew; he had a piece of string with leaves hanging on it.

There were cold storage rooms you could walk into, lined with thick cork; some were for storing ice, some for poultry and some for meat for local butchers and poultry

Venables family, Minn End 1953

Ladies Guild garden party at Minn End Farm Bosley.
Mrs Thompstone, Yvonne Needham, Arthur Venables, Eleanor Venables, Kathleen Hadfield,
Front: Charles Needham, Rev. Cecil Watkinson and his sister Mrs Kenyon.

dealers, anyone who wanted cold storage. After the war as fridges became the norm in butchers shops that trade died so I converted the factory to a body shop and sold all the equipment but retained the overhead running crane, using that in the car repair business.

I was the first one around here to have an alignment jig for repairing smashed up cars. All our cars were

Tony Riha, German POW working for Tom Goodwin at Morris Green Farm

repaired to manufacturers' specifications - no guesswork. We were very busy and trained nearly two dozen men over the years. There is a dammed up pool in Whittakers Field at Mill House Farm from which water ran a turbine which generated all our electricity.

The station was a very good hunting ground for us for the repair trade; cars had to go over a level crossing by Wood Treatment and in those days the Mini was very low and the railway track was too high so if they went down too fast it smashed the bottom of the car up.

I married Una in 1952 and we lived at Rosedale where after a few years she ran a cafe. I remember when they were building the GPO tower the men used to come down to it for something to eat.

During our married life of 60 years we spent 25 of them over the hill in Wildboarclough but its nice to be back at my birthplace although I never felt that I left; we returned to Bosley Chapel every week which is where we met on Good Friday 1942.

The present Bosley Methodist Chapel was built in 1885. Our family were Methodists and every Sunday we went to the Sunday school (in our best clothes). It was very well attended in those days; each scholar was given a book prize every year for good attendance and an annual trip to the seaside by coach was organised by the teachers.

We had a walking round Sunday every June singing a hymn at each house and inviting everyone to the Sunday school Anniversary services on the following Sunday.

Every Christmas we took part in the traditional carol singing which covered the whole village. All money collected was given to the National Childrens Homes; this has been done by Bosley Methodists for over one hundred years and still exists today on a smaller scale. Each Good Friday we had an afternoon tea followed by a religious concert with items by the Sunday school scholars and teenagers. This is where I met Una, my future wife - the best prize I ever had!

The graveyard was acquired from Mr Fallows of Key Green Farm and consisted of one acre of ground which was consecrated for burials in the year 1921.

Hilda Leach

I have memories of walking round Sunday at chapel. We sang at all the houses and stopped for swiss buns and lemonade at the home of my parents, Mr and Mrs Frank Buxton. Other great days were prize-giving for good attendance; I still have the books and also the sermons where we all had a new frock. There would be two rows of children on the stage.

For a time there was a club for boys in the Queens garden; they played billiards and the tennis club was for a short time in George Goodwin's field near the bridge in the works. Then it was at the vicarage in Mr Babbington's days as vicar. He was a strange character; he wore a straw boater and his head was always on one side. But if any children went to his door there was always an apple or orange for them.

Miss Cheetham the village postman had a long uniform and a cocked hat. As she approached the house she would burst into song. Her nephew, Leslie was the church organist.

At school we sat at long desks with a form behind and played in the playground with no supervision. I picked violets from the hedgerow on my way home.

I was told that my great grandfather turned the mill in the works from a copper mill to a corn mill. He was Robert Brindley, relative of James Brindley. Unfortunately he was drunk when he signed over the mill to Thompstone.

Higher Works, Bosley pre 1901.
The tramlines were dug up for the War effort in 1940

Bishop of Chester consecrating Churchyard extension

Bosley Church Choir 1936
Back: Tom Coates, Fred Oakden, Tom Cox, Norris Arnold, Percy Owen, Fred Norbury, Harry Mayer, Denis --
Doris Mayer, May Owen, Sidney Cleaver (organist), Rev. Lloyd Jones and his wife, and Lydia Franklin
Front: George Goodwin, Joe, Leslie and Sybil Arnold

Frances Jeffries

I was born in 1920, the third of four daughters of Frank and Annie Simpson of Old School House, Bosley. My sisters were Mary, Annie and Irene. Next door to us lived the Miss Coxons - Miss Coxon the elder and Blanch who was born with a muscular illness; she was in a wheelchair all her life and was unable to walk or feed herself. Nadens lived in the bottom house; they were the parents of Charlie Burns's wife who lived just below the school.

Dad had a shed behind the house where he made clogs and mended shoes for people. Mr Peter Yates who owned the Harrington Arms bought some Hereford beef cattle to supply his Wine Lodge restaurants in Blackpool and Manchester. Dad and Mr Tom Lawton slaughtered them when needed. Mr Yates only wanted the best cuts so dad and Mr Lawton divided the rest between them. Mother was a good cook so we had roast heart, liver and potato pies made in a big enamel bowl. I loved the brains which are now no longer offered for sale.

North Rode

In 1929 when Mary was 14 she left school and went to work at Brocklehurst, Whistons silk mill in Macclesfield. She had to walk to North Rode Station to catch the 7am train to Macclesfield then walk to the mill in Hurdsfield to start work at 8 o'clock. She worked till 6pm then had to retrace her journey home.

Mrs Mather

Annie passed the 11plus to go to the Central School at Macclesfield; she had to catch the 8 o'clock train to Macclesfield then walk from the station to the school in Byrons Street. In 1930 we moved to Macclesfield.

I started school in 1925; we were taught by Mrs Mather in the small schoolroom while Mr Mather taught the older children in the big room. We wrote on slates with grey pencils. While I was in the infants class Miss Coxon died and on the day of the funeral I could hear the horses coming down the road. I wanted to see them going down the slope opposite the school into the churchyard so I stood up. Mrs Mather made me stand on a form till home-time as punishment.

On Empire Day we went into the schoolyard where the Union Jack was flying. We gathered round it and sang patriotic songs, we saluted the flag and had a half day holiday.

In the winter a concert party came to the school in the evening; I remember George Hoy and Darkie Swindells, Doris Wellings and Dorothy Joule with Billy Williams the comedian. The partition was taken down and a stage erected. We all paid fourpence; the place was packed, the lads sitting on the window-sills. I remember walking home in a group on a moonlit frosty night looking at the stars.

I remember going to church on Sunday mornings; Mr Babbington was the vicar. The lady who kept the Post Office, Miss Lucy Cheetham was very tall and straight and a keen disciplinarian. One morning someone came late to the service and I turned round. Before I got home Miss Cheetham had been up to tell my mother that I had turned round in church! Mrs Carter who moved into the schoolhouse when Mr Mather went to live in the bungalow took the Sunday School along with Margaret Coates. One year she produced *Red Riding Hood* and we all took part; we had a stage and curtains.

Every year we went on the Sunday school trip to the seaside - Southport, Rhyl or Llandudno in a charabanc; for most of us it was the only time we saw the sea. With dinner and tea provided it was a real treat. At Southport we were told if we got lost to go to Salts Cafe where we were having tea.

Bosley vicarage

The organ was played by Sydney Cleaver whose father kept the clog shop in Macclesfield where dad got his materials for making clogs. He came with Tom Cox who sang in the choir; they married the Clayton girls who came to church - Sydney married Helen and Tom married Winnie who used to bring her dog to church; I was terrified of it. We decorated the church for harvest; we children gathered rose hips and threaded them with a darning needle and thin string into lengths to festoon the font.

Dad played in Bosley cricket team; they played in a field opposite the chapel against visiting teams and Mr Babbington started a tennis club on the vicarage lawn.

In the winter when it froze hard the reservoir would freeze over and at weekends people came to skate on it. One day Grandfather, James Simpson, who lived in Bosley Works went to skate on his own. He arrived at our house dripping wet and freezing cold. He had gone through the ice but had managed to pull himself out. Mother had been baking so she opened the oven door, sat grandad on a chair as near as she could get him and wrapped him in a blanket. He was nearly 70 at the time. When they dismantled the flour mill at Bosley he went to watch and some machinery went through an upper floor; he was underneath and escaped with 2 broken big toes. He lived to be 92.

I remember steam wagons towing Collins Fair from Macclesfield to Leek every May and October and the drovers walking the cattle to market. One day we had some hunger marchers; they stopped by our gate and mother made them all a drink. Their shoes were worn out; they were going to London.

Catherine Bradley

My introduction to Bosley was through a young man of 17 who I met on my first day of work; he already worked at Brocklehurst Whiston Silk Mill in Macclesfield. I knew as I looked into his extremely blue eyes that I would marry him and several years later after the war, I did.

Syd eventually asked me to go out with him and meet his very good friends Mr and Mrs Appleton who lived down by Wood Treatment Mill in Bosley Higher Works. I borrowed my friends bicycle and set off to meet Syd at Moss Rose, for in those days I had never been further than St Barnabus Church and I may have got lost without his help.

It wasn't a very romantic outing for just after meeting up with each other the heavens opened and the rain poured down. I had a short mac on but my stockings got glued to my knees and with pedalling my knees popped through two big holes which steadily got bigger. I have never felt so ashamed of my appearance but due to my father being very strict and me having to wear everything three inches below my knees my hosts didn't seem to notice anything other than two young, wet people.

Mr Appleton offered us a drink of sherry to warm us up; I didn't know how to tell Syd that I had never had sherry - never mind that there was a big moth floating on the top so I took a deep breath, shut my eyes and downed the drink and managed to keep the moth out of my mouth. We sat at the table in front of a roaring fire and ate ham and tomatoes with bread and butter followed with damsons and cream but because the fruit dish did not have a flat edge for me to put the stones on, I swallowed all seven of them!

My next visit to Bosley was after the war when Syd asked me to go and meet his family. He did say that his mother ran a cafe but I didn't realise that I was expected to wait on tables, wash up and chat to cyclists who were drying off their socks on the fireguard and putting their cigarettes out in the plant pots and totally ignoring the ash trays. I didn't know then that I had begun something that would take up most of my waking hours after I got married.

It was 1949 when we were allocated a council house in Bosley; these were primarily built for farmers and men who had been in the services and whose family came from Bosley. We were given No 3 Lakeside. Mr and Mrs Harold Murfin lived at No 1, Mr and Mrs Harold Yoxall at No 5, Mr and Mrs Frank Marlow at No 7, Mr and Mrs George Jones at No 9 and Mr and Mrs Arthur Jones in No 11. Across the road were Mr and Mrs Brown at No 8, Mr and Mrs Woodward at No 6, Mr and Mrs Wade at No 4 and Mr and Mrs Vernon Williamson at No 2. We were all newcomers and soon got to know each other well as our children walked off to school together, came home together and played together; it was a lovely place to live; so peaceful and happy.

The houses had three outbuildings - one contained a wash-house with sink and coal fuelled boiler in the corner. We used to rise at 5am and light the boiler and give the clothing in the dolly tub another good possing that had been put in the night before to help soak the dirt out. Later it was transferred into the boiler and boiled for half an hour, rinsed in cold water and hung out on the line to dry. It was wonderful to see clean clothes blowing in the wind and to smell the freshness when they were dry. It was very different if it started to rain for everything would be covered in sooty spots from the smoky fires and all would need washing again.

The coal house was attached to the wash-house; there was no door or lock, it was open but no-one stole anything in those days. Next to that was the outside toilet which was a God-send for it saved the children running up and down the stairs every time they needed to use it. There was a small passage between the house and the out houses and because of the strong winds in winter we decided to put a door each end of the passage which also kept the snow out and away from the back door.

When all the new residents arrived I can still see how thrilled we all were to have been given the chance of a large three bedroomed house with a bathroom; no more bringing in the tin bath off the house wall and filling it to bathe one after the other, cleanest first, topping up the water from the boiler contained in the fire surround, getting into our night clothes in front of the fire then mum and dad would carry it outside and pour the water down the outside drain. Cosy but a lot of work.

In the kitchen were yards and yards of copper pipes all of which I carefully cleaned with pride until my son was born then it became a chore. There was a wonderful north facing larder with a cold slab; nothing ever went bad however long we kept it for there were no refrigerators then. After a year we had all got our gardens into shape and my husband planted a fir tree that still stands to this day. We all grew our own vegetables and soft fruit trees.

I personally didn't need the services of Jacksons for I made all my own bread and cakes but was very pleased to have Dennis Spearings Meat Van to call. That was driven by Mr Kirk, a very patient person who had a chat with us, made us laugh and served us well. There were also the Wardle Brothers who came with clothing which we could buy on weekly instalments. The Co-op van came with groceries.

In those days we had a good bus service going from the Harrington Arms into Macclesfield or at the end of the little cottages on the roadside to go into Leek or Derby. There was the school bus around 8.45am and back to Macclesfield at 4pm with a 2 hourly service in between. The trains went from North Rode every hour.

On visiting the little Post Office which was run then by Miss Warrington who looked after her invalid mother I was asked if I would be interested in forming a Ladies Guild. I remember at the initial meeting there were seven people; Mrs Franklin, Mrs Hadfield, Mrs Yarwood, Mrs Goodfellow, Mrs Dines, Miss Warrington and myself. Gradually week by week more people came and we had some good speakers, discussions and eventually we put on a concert for the village.

During the war Bosley had its own fire brigade and Syd used to be allowed to go out with them; he wasn't really old enough but he was very tall and strong but above all he enjoyed the thrill of it.

On Sunday afternoons we often walked along the banks of the reservoir and had a picnic. One day we had just taken our shoes and socks off ready to paddle in the feeder when we heard the thundering of horses hooves. We ran across the stream, I pushed the children through a gap in the hedge and there was this huge stallion rearing up on its hind legs and flaying the air with its front legs. The children were terrified - I quickly picked up a pebble and aimed for the Lucozade bottle and prayed. Fortunately the pebble hit the bottle and it exploded which frightened the horse and it galloped off. I quickly tied up the blanket with everything in it, shoes, socks and broken bottle, and headed for home.

In 1952 Syd brought home a Peto-Scott television set for Christmas; what a novelty that was - pictures in our own home. We had all the children who lived on the estate in watching Andy Pandy, The Flowerpot Men and Muffin the Mule. When Syd came home we listened quietly to the news; the news readers dressed in dinner jackets and they spoke the Queens English. There were even people telling us we just had time to make a cup of tea or watch the horses plough a field or look at the potters wheel turning. We heard that Queen Elizabeth was going to be crowned and it would be on the television. Everyone was given a day off work and so we invited all the people on the estate to come into our home and watch it providing they all brought a chair to sit on.

Syd lined everyone up like in a cinema; I provided steak and kidney pie, potatoes and vegetables followed with rice pudding. We all had a wonderful day together ending with a cup of tea and a cake. On going home lots of them asked me to bake for them so on the following day I asked Mrs Dines if I could rent her outhouse and pay her to start off selling cakes and pies because the council at that time would not allow residents to have a business in their property.

By the weekend Mrs Dines was selling her own Swiss buns and cakes; I didn't realise at the time that I had been talking to a Master Baker. This was the beginning of the local village shop at Fresh Winds.

Mrs Mason and Syd's new stepfather had just finished having a house built and decided to open it up as a cafe to help pay off the mortgage. They called the house Hurst Lea. During the first few years we had no-one but cyclists then an AA man used to call every Friday then we got two or three coaches going from Derby to Blackpool. The drivers would ring to tell us they were on their way and we (me, Mrs Mason and Aunty Mary) would butter three or four loaves of bread, make sandwiches and place them in the larder on trays covered with a tea towel then warm two huge brown teapots and as soon as the coach arrived the driver got out, took a tray of sandwiches onto the coach and pass them round then come in again, take in cups and one of us would follow with the tea while the driver went in and had his.

Slowly cars came along and motor cycles and the trade really took off. Aunty Mary and Syd were paid £3 a week and I got 6 eggs. Over the years Mrs Mason built a really lovely home, beautifully furnished and took me to Hanley to buy clothes for my children as they came along. She also started the caravan site off with permission for 6 vans and 6 tents. The place has been altered a lot and is now called Boars Leigh and has static homes on the site.

When Mr Greenacre, the vicar, left, Mr Watkinson and his sister Mrs Kenyon came to the vicarage. They worked hard at getting the people together; he started off the bell ringing again for during the war the bells had only been used as a warning that an Air Raid was coming. I remember he used to toll the bell just five minutes before we were due in church. Different choir boys used to pump up the organ for the hymns and when they got tired or forgot, the organ droned to a halt. Eventually we had a full set of bell ringers and the sound of bells for Church and weddings was wonderfully uplifting.

Mrs Kenyon came round the village and got the ladies interested in joining the Mothers Union and although the vicarage was a draughty and cold place, it was always warm for our meetings. Mr Moody came to the church from Wildboarclough and he started a choir. Like everything else it was hard work to find anyone interested but with perseverance we formed a really good choir. He told me I had a good voice and asked

The restoration of the bells

Rev. Lloyd Jones with the bellringers at the anniversary of the restoration of the bells 1935.
Back: Fred Oakden, Tom Coates, Jack Simpson, Percy Owen, Norris Arnold, Harry Mayer, Horace Marsden
Front: Rachel Goodfellow, Frank Goodfellow, Bob Pownall, Rev Lloyd Jones, - -, - -

me to sing solos then Mrs Kenyon came to our house and asked me if I felt I could do a nativity play for the children. I loved children and enjoyed making up costumes and plays for them to perform and did this until I left the village.

Mrs Kenyon was also responsible for starting off the Rose Queen. I told her I could not fit any more into my busy life then found myself saying yes, if it was only going to be once a year! The first Queen was Pamela Bradley, my husband's niece. Her mother bought the material and I made her dress and the dresses of some of the attendants. Mrs Kenyon provided the lovely velvet train.

It was a very successful day for Mrs Dines had been persuaded to have a cake stall and Mrs Hadfield sold refreshments and Miss Roberts held sports events for the children. As years went on Mr Holland came into the village and he began to hold a tug of war event which started the world famous Bosley Tug of War Team.

In 1985 I was asked if I would open the Rose Queen and Sports Day event to celebrate its 30th anniversary. There were twenty previous Queens able to attend and Miss Marlow was that year's Queen.

I was saddened to hear later on that year that the council had decided to demolish the existing Airey Houses because faults had been found in ones which were built in Yorkshire. Mr Whittaker's field nearby had been bought for the construction of 14 smaller semi-detached houses and six semi-detached bungalows. By doing this the council altered the warm feeling of friendliness to one of frustration and anger and as a visitor I felt glad I had lived in Bosley for the first ten years of the first council estate there and also the fact that I had

helped along with Syd, his aunty Mary and my mother-in-law to build Hurst Lea into a flourishing business. I was a founder member of the Ladies Guild, Mothers Union, Village Shop, Rose Queen and Sports Day and the Church Choir - I never did get the hang of bell ringing. What a wonderful life we had in Bosley thanks to the efforts of people like Mrs Kenyon, Mr Watkinson, Mr Moody and all the ladies they roped in to start things off.

Tennis Club 1920s with Rev Babbington

Bosley Flower Sermons

Bosley Ladies, surnames only
Back: Nixon, Marsden, Mold, Arnold, Cook, Mitchell
Buxton, Shaw, Heapy, Simpson, Tatton, Naden, Marsden, Cheetham
Front: Mrs Booth, Mrs Mather, Mrs O'Brien, Mrs Thompstone, Bullock, Roe

Freda Owen

I was evacuated from West Gorton in Manchester in 1941 and I was taken in by Mr and Mrs Pownall who lived at Penn Bridge. Mrs Pownall picked me up from Bosley School after I had travelled on the train to Macclesfield with other children from the Manchester area. All the local children wore clogs so my mother bought me some red ones. After always wearing shoes I found it very different wearing clogs.

My mum and dad worked on munitions so they only came to see me once a month. Each time they came they went to Shuker's and Whittaker's farms to buy fresh eggs to take back to Manchester for the family there. My cousin Norma was staying on a farm near to Bosley Crossroads and I used to go on my bike to see her. I also used to visit Cynthia's grandma who lived at the Nurses Cottage.

There were lot of children from my school in West Gorton who came to stay with families in Bosley. Teachers from our city school used to travel to Bosley to help out with our lessons and they also made sure that we were all happy in the country. It was a big change for a city child to walk for miles through fields and to play in streams.

Ernest Whittaker at Mill Farm

Main Road near Minn End Lane

Bosley School 1947

Bosley School

Cicely Mason, Cathy Gibson, Winnie Heath, --, Sister Mary?, Eva Hine, Rachael Simpson, Dennis Bradley, Bill Robinson
2nd Freda Cheetham, Frances Buxton, Barbara Knight, Barbara Lawson, Nelly Burns, Miriam Hadfield, Alice Hargreaves
Bill Hargreaves, Leslie Cheetham, --, Tom Coates, Harold Yoxall
3rd May Robinson, Rene Moores, Daisy Hine, Sister Annie, Mabel Nadin, Hilda Buxton, Margery Burns, Leonard Gould,
Fred Vahden, Tom Goodwin, Dennis Moss, Harry Bradley, Jim Slack, --
Front: - Simpson, Margery Lawson, Gertie Gould, - Eaton, Joan Mason, Jessie Jones, Mary Slack,
Daphne Knight, --, Sydney Bullock

**Bosley School
1966-67**

1947 Infants boys
Back:
- -, Robert Nicklin

Front:
Brian Mitchell, - -,
Brian Gerrard,
- Marlow, Peter
Marlow, - -,
Graham Owen

1947 Infants girls

- Marlow, Ellen Franklin, - -, Pamela Jones, Janice Hartley, - -, - -, Kathleen Venables

1947
Joe Beech?,
Malcolm Knight,
Ernest Whittaker,
- -, Anson
Franklin, Arthur
Gibson

1947 Senior Girls

Back:
Frances Venables, Cynthia Pownall, Joyce Angel, Phyllis Beech, Sylvia Nicklin

Front:
Barbara Gerrard, Lilian Heath, Hannah Goodfellow, ?Jean Coates, Freda Gilman, Margaret Needham

Kathleen Mason seated 2nd from left, 2nd row

Bosley Sunday School 1920s

Front
Elsie Bowyer, Barbara Lawson, Marjorie Burns, Maria Hargreaves, Gertie Gould, Frances Simpson, Joyce Shelley

Back
Alice Hargreaves, Mary Coates, Rene Moores, Mary Simpson, Freda Cheetham, Annie Simpson, Nellie Burns

Behind
Margaret Coates, Mrs Carter, Rev. Babbington

Me and Him at the Harrington Arms, Bosley. Cynthia Edwards

Me, Cynthia and Him, Cyril, took over the management of the Harrington Arms in 1967. It was hard work at the start because Cyril was recovering from amoebiasis which

had resulted from his National Service in Malaya where he had amoebic dysentery. We found the work areas okay but the living areas were in a dreadful state. They were so bad that my mother refused to let our sons move in with us until they had been made habitable. Our employers Yates Brothers Wine Lodges made a huge effort to make our living quarters better so that we could be a family again.

During the following 16 years we saw many changes in our clientele, the quality of our bar staff and kitchen staff were a big part of these changes. One of the downstairs rooms was converted from a living room into a catering kitchen and this started a new kind of clientele who repeatedly came back for more.

We used to organise many activities to raise money for Guide Dogs for the Blind and other local charities and for many years we organised a day out to the Grand National which was always a grand day out. It was the happy memories of these outings that resulted in Cyril's ashes being scattered by the 'Chair' at Aintree.

Harrington Harvest Auction
Phyllis Poole,
Cynthia Edwards,
Margaret Gibson,
Cyril Edwards,
Mike Bennett,
George Poole

As with many companies the management and staff changed and with that came changing ideas; although we were generating good financial results the company decided that it was time for a change in management for the Harrington and this resulted in me and him leaving our happy memories behind and moving on in 1983.

Bosley Reservoir

In 1978 Cheshire Conservation Trust, now Cheshire Wildlife Trust, published a booklet called *A Lake in the Hills*. The authors were Oxenham and Tunnicliffe. The following information is taken from this publication with permission of CWT.

On 9th November 1831 the Macclesfield Canal was opened when a procession of 25 boats from the north and 52 from the south met at Macclesfield. As many as 800 workmen had been involved in the construction and that day 500 workmen and 200 boatmen and drivers were each given half a crown to spend as they pleased.

The canal is 26 miles long and cost £320,000 which included the cost of constructing the reservoir. Bosley locks were regarded as probably the finest locks in the country and the stone to build them came from the Cloud, Stoneyfold and Gawsworth Common quarries. Covering 86 acres the reservoir held 402 million gallons of water - equivalent of 11,000 locks of water. One operation of a wide lock could use 60,000 gallons of water but with each lock having a side pond, the water taken from the canal was halved and after Sutton Reservoir was completed in 1838 the canal company was able to add to its revenues by selling surplus water. Between 1844 and 1846 it sold 200 million gallons at 2d per 1000 gallons to keep Manchester's Gorton Reservoir full.

Provision had to be made to keep the Bosley and Swallowdale brooks flowing normally to the mill downstream, and to the Dane, so feeders were constructed. These are also known as lades or conduits.

The canal was not the success anticipated; the railways proved its undoing and in 1846 the Macclesfield Canal Co. was taken over by the Sheffield, Ashton-under-Lyne and Manchester Railway Co. ending with the formation of British Railways in 1948. British Waterways took over the canal in 1962 including the reservoir.

Some of the land around the reservoir remained in the possession of the lord of the manor, the Earl of Harrington, who in 1859 built a new house called Highfield House for the Broster family. Following the death of the eighth earl in 1917 the ninth earl was obliged to sell most of his Bosley and Gawsworth estates to meet death duties and in 1920 at auction, Mr Yates bought the island on Bosley Reservoir and the reservoir sporting rights for £2300 plus £50 for timber valuation. He also bought the Harrington Arms and 25 acres for £2463.

An interesting comment is recorded from the book *Mereside Chronicle* by the artist C.F. Tunnicliffe who tells of a grebe that persisted in building its nest near to the Waterman's house and sitting tight even though there were never any eggs in the nest. Puzzled by this Tunnicliffe accepted the Watermans explanation that the grebe was barren though it was alleged that the truth was that every time the bird laid an egg the Waterman took it for breakfast!

A more detailed account, including the natural history and references, can be found on a link from Wikipedia

Arthur Gibson, Margaret Massey

Our grandparents came from Bucklow near to Wilmslow. They moved to Styal where Aunty Kathleen was born in 1915 then they came to Bosley to an old cottage called Reservoir Cottage, then in 1917 Swallowdale Lodge was built and they moved in there.

Swallowdale Lodge

Grandad had a horse and trap and grandma would go shopping at Congleton with it. Coming back the horse wouldn't go past the Robin Hood, he wanted to pull in because Grandad must have been in the habit of stopping there. She used to complain when she got home that she'd been shown up.

Dad was a farmhand; he went out to Australia in 1926 until 1933. He used to tell us about driving the horses with loads of corn to the station at night because it was cooler.

At home they farmed in a small way but grandad wasn't well and died in 1937 so dad had to take it all on. It was only a sideline really because he was the Waterman; the water bailiff. He looked after Bosley Reservoir, Turks Head Reservoir at Sutton and all the feeders down to the canal and up the Shell Brook Feeder and Swallowdale to Turks Head. By the time he'd walked round the reservoir and up and down the feeders he had plenty to occupy him and that was after he'd milked the ten cows or so at home and done the calves and pigs and then again when he came home.

He had to keep all the feeders running and look after the sluices. If the water level was down in the canal he had to let more water through from the valve at the dam head. A lot of stuff like coal went by the canal then. When he was cleaning the feeders out he used to stand in them and dig them out by hand. He did all the hedge cutting and scything out. The only tools he had were scythe, shovel and slashing hook for the hedges. He used to walk the feeders with a shovel on his shoulder then he'd loosen anything that was made up. When the wood was felled below Franklin's farm a lot of ground slipped and went into the Feeder and dad had to dig it out.

At one time British Rail owned the reservoir and they wouldn't let dad run any

Plough Sunday Bosley Church, 1950s

**Bob Heathcote (left) started his milk round in 1949 and it ran until the end of churn collection
Here picking up from Fryers at Park House Farm, Horton**

water off. He said there was always a fortnight of winter then when he didn't go to bed because it was that full and water would be lapping over the top. He would be walking about with a lantern in case the dam head went - I don't know what he thought he'd do, he'd got no telephone or anything! When it changed to British Waterways it was fine.

Because of the rail link dad always had a railway pass and when we were kids our day's holiday was going to Belle Vue Zoo on the train. There were five of us children - Arthur, Malcolm, Margaret, Jean and Irene. There was no electric and just a cold water tap. We used to go to school on the milk wagon; he seemed to pile a few kids on everywhere - a few in the front and others hanging onto the rail on the back. He stopped at Buxtons where we clambered off and walked over the hill to the school. Some of Coopers drivers were Harry Cotterill, Sammy Mottershead and Ted Myatt.

Miss Roberts, who taught us, her grandfather was captain of the ship that David Livingstone went in and she had a number of his artefacts. When it was the Coronation we went to her house to see it on her television. A lot of people have commented that anyone taught by Miss Roberts has never gone wrong; she had very high moral standards. As soon as it was nice weather at school it was desks outside and you had your lessons outside and we went on nature walks, down the fields towards Wood Treatment or round the reservoir. We didn't know a lot of history but we knew our maths, we were very religious, we knew the bible and we knew nature. We learned a legend about the Giants Footstep on Bosley Cloud and one on Shutlingsloe. By the one on the Cloud are some little footsteps supposed to be of a mouse which frightened the giant away.

In wartime there were thick cables strung across the reservoir with chestnut palings and drums hung on. The posts are still there on the reservoir ground which they fastened them to. You could stand on the cables and there was a Pillbox at Top Bridge. - Jim Warren was the lengthsman. He had a smallholding up at Bosley Brooks and fed his animals on what he cut from the verges.

Dad used to make some hay on tripods; he would put some brush down then this wooden frame and layer the hay over it. There is an old hayshed which must be a hundred years old still there which is unusual because it has a roof of thin lead sheets.

We remember him saying he used to walk to Flash Market where they bought some stock and walked them back. Grandfather used to rent some ground down by the sawdust mill by the Dane and they walked them down there. By that time the cattle were exhausted; they would have also been walked into the market earlier in the day.

Mr and Mrs Frank Whittaker and the Vicar

Evelyn Twigg (nee Trelfa)

My grandparents, Ezra Worthington and Jane Potts both worked at Shellow Farm, Gawsworth; Ezra was a cowman and Jane a servant. They lived at The Thatched Cottage, High lane, Gawsworth where their first son Horace was born. They moved to Top Lock Cottage, Canal Side, Bosley in 1884 and my grandfather was the lock keeper to 12 locks in the Cheshire Ring.

They had ten children in a three bedroom house and they had some land where they kept cows and hens to give the family milk and eggs. My mother, Edna Worthington was born at Top Lock in 1925. Ezra retired in 1927 aged 65.

All the children attended North Rode School and they walked to school through the park. They remembered seeing their first car which was owned by Tootal Broadhurst who lived at The Manor; the boys raised their caps and the girls had to curtsey.

My mother and her two sisters went out to be domestic servants in Macclesfield. They earned their keep and saved 6d a week for their train fares. My father worked as a lengthsman working from Bosley 12th Lock to Buxton Road Bridge; he had to do hedge cutting and reed pulling amongst other jobs.

I started at St Marys School, Bosley on 19th May 1930. I walked across two fields to Lower House Farm and then I walked with Leslie, Sybil and Joe Arnold up their old cart road and came out onto the main Leek road above the Harrington Arms and on to the school with our packed lunch.

At school, tea and cocoa were brewed on the fire in a big iron kettle. I was in Mrs Lindop's class; she travelled from Hanley every day by train. She walked through the fields from the station to the school along with the children from Higher Works. We all had three sweets on a Friday; Mrs Lindop was a lovely teacher. At the age of ten we all went into the Big Room to Mrs Lomax who was followed by Mrs Hopgood who lived next door to the school. She made a garden in the boys playground where we all worked doing hoeing and weeding and we grew vegetables. We went on nature walks and had sports days in Mr and Mrs Gould's field.

I remember the Christmas party gifts off the big tree and the cinematograph films of Charlie Chaplin shown by Mr Walter Brown from the Harrington House. He also gave us all a gift - a cup and saucer or handkerchiefs. I remember his funeral; all the school children lined up in the churchyard. He was placed in a vault by the church door.

Some of the children in Standard 2 passed the 11 plus and went to either the Central School or the High School in Macclesfield. I stayed on at Bosley until August 1939; the 2nd World War started and I was fourteen years old.

I started work in September at Warburtons shop, cafe and bakehouse on Waters Green, Macclesfield; my wage was £2 a week. I walked up the canal to the 5th Lock, walked along Station Road to North Rode Railway Station to get the 8am steam train. I met up with my school friends who had got on the train at Bosley; they worked in the mills making war clothes etc. I worked until 4pm in the blackout days.

We girls enjoyed the dances at Bosley, North Rode, Eaton and Timbersbrook. We paid 2 shillings a night, 8pm to 1am. We all walked in a gang in snow, rain and wind under a pitch black sky with our torches. We wore black to get there and then got all dressed up in the cloakroom. Great days!!

Minnie and Norris Arnold c.1923

Arnold family

**Norris Arnold,
Bosley Show**

**Lower House
Farm**

To get to Timbersbrook I walked through the Tram Wood to meet up with the girls from the Works then we walked up to Bosley Cloud. The Tram Wood was where the steam train took the wood flour from the canal to Bosley Mill. The boats were unloaded from the 12th Lock; there could be 30 boats lined up waiting to be unloaded. The canal was very busy at that time.

The Tram Wood was beautiful when the bluebells and primroses were on the railway embankment on the Churnet Valley Line. The LMS railway passed Lower Lock and I remember watching the trains carrying troops, prisoners of war and evacuees. I watched coal wagons and pleasure trip trains off to Rudyard Lake, Leek and Uttoxeter.

The canal was very busy; boats used to carry pots, coal, sauces etc. Father used to help with the ice boat by being a rocker on the platform of the boat pulled by two horses hired from Mr Biddulph of Bell Farm, North Rode. The pay was 7/6d a day for man and horse. They pulled the boat to Congleton and then came back on the train. Back next morning to Congleton and on to Mow Cop and back on the train at night. This was repeated over four days until they returned to Bosley. The horses were stabled on route. The Marple team did likewise from Top Lock, Marple to Top Lock, Bosley. The 12 locks were flushed to break the 6-8 inches ice with walls of snow 3 feet high.

The boat horses were stabled at Lower Lock at 6d a night. We paid rent for house and stable to the canal company at about 5 shillings a week. My father's wage was 30 shillings a week rising to £2 a week with overtime when he had to sit up at night when it was raining very heavily to raise the paddle at the overflow to stop Congleton Locks being flooded. The water entered the River Dane at No 12 Lock.

Father had a vegetable garden and five damson trees. He sold fishing tickets and my mother brewed tea for fishermen; a jug of tea and cups for 6d a brew. We had no water or electricity, just oil lamps and candles. We carried water from two wells, one near the River Dane a quarter of a mile away and one at no 11 lock. We got paraffin oil, bread etc from Coopers at no 5 lock.

Mother's brother, Charles Worthington, lived at Canal Side Cottage at Buglawton; he was the ganger and delivered the mens'' wages each week and delivered time sheets and collected them from Marple office. He also collected notice board news which was posted on a bill board on Lower and Top Lock Cottages; I think all the cottages had one.

My family lived at Lower Lock for 18 years; in 1945 my father died aged 46 and mother and I had to leave and go and live with her father, aged 84 and blind, who lived in Wardle Crescent, Gawsworth. Another canal employee went to live at Lower Lock Cottage. With Canal Cottage it was knocked down in 1963. Top Lock remains but it was sold and extended and sold again in 1990 for £110. In 1947 I married Harry Twigg and we lived at Ridge Hall Farm, Sutton before moving into Macclesfield.

Near Chaff Hall
Jan 1940

Leslie Heath

I was born in 1933 at Woodside Farm on Cloudside; my mother and father were Clifford and Emma Heath nee Bullock. I was the oldest having two sisters, Lilian and Winifred and a brother John. I used to walk to Bosley School; it was about a mile and a half and being wartime I had to carry my lunch and a gas mask with me.

On Sundays we went to morning service at Bosley Methodist Church then walked to Sunday school in the afternoon. The teachers were Mr Charles Needham who was my uncle and Mr George Naden. I attended until I was 19.

Evening service was attended by a good number of teenagers; this was our weekly get together. In summer we cycled miles. Every Good Friday we put on a concert where we performed plays and sketches and sang songs and anthems with the choir. At Christmas we went carol singing around the village to raise money for the National Children's Home.

When I left school I worked on the farm helping my father. I learned to milk the cows and work with the two horses, Bonnie and Kit. After a year father bought a second-hand David Brown tractor which made work easier. We grew potatoes to sell locally and ox cabbage, swedes and mangolds were grown for winter feed for the cows. We also grew barley and oats which were cut with a binder. This made sheaves which we had to stook in the field before carting to the barn where it was later thrashed. The grain was put through a hammer mill and ground down for cattle feed.

In 1954 dad bought Lower Key Green Farm. We kept 33 cows and 20 youngstock. Dad also bought a muckspreader and hay baler to make life easier. Having electricity, mother bought a washing machine and cooker; we thought it was great to be able to flick a switch and have light.

In 1959 John left school and came to work on the farm. We started to keep a lot of laying hens and dad went on his first holiday with mother. Sadly in 1960 dad died from a heart attack aged 55. John and I carried on farming until he bought a farm. I continued at Key Green until I retired and our son David now farms it.

Peter Whittaker at Mill House Farm

Early days TOW at Rushton

Bill Nixon   Norman Biddulph   Tom Sumner   Bill & Ivy Biddulph

1950 Back: J. Cook, Arthur Bailey, Jim Dandy, Alex Brown, Sam Holland
Front: Arthur Brown, George Oliver, Joe Cotterill

Bosley Tug of War

In the later 1940s Alex Brown had a Tug of War team which consisted mainly of farmers who were customers of John Cook Snr, the local corn merchant. He became interested through visiting them on training nights and they made him president. The team was known as Cookies Eight and pulled under this name for a few years.

They changed their name to Bosley Farmers as they took the sport more seriously and were also known as Men of Oak because their training method at one time was to pull on a rope around the branch of a very large oak tree with a system of pulleys attached to 18 milk churns filled with sand which weighed a ton. By raising and holding this up many times, they did their training.

The club became a member of the Amateur Athletic Association, the 3As, and became very successful travelling all over the country competing. To help with expenses, in 1957 the firm of Bosley Wood Treatment became the patron. The AAA Championship was held at White City and in 1959 the Wood Treatment Bosley team won the Catchweight Championship title and then again for the following 20 years.

The team went on to have great success; Sam Holland was the coach for 17 years and they had a new training ground in a field next to his garage from where he ran a milk lorry haulage business. The men often trained here by 4 men pulling against another 4 and holding. The record for a hold with neither side gaining ground was 17 minutes. Intense training paid off with the team winning the Catchweight and 100 stone AAA Title in 1962. This was followed by a total of 32 3As Titles, 32 TOW Association outdoor National Titles, 24 Indoor and 11 Inter County and 2 UK Championships.

In the early 1900s the sport was an Olympic event and Britain won gold medals. Some people were interested in raising the profile of TOW again so in 1960 an International Federation was formed. In 1964 a European Championship at 720kg was held in Sweden and Bosley as National Champions went to compete.... and win. In 1972 South Africa became the first non European Country to join TWIF and so WT Bosley and Camberly were invited to represent England at 720 and 640kg on a 17 day tour there.

In Holland in 1975, TWIF staged the first ever World ToW Championship and WT Bosley won gold medals. In 1976 in South Africa, the world saw the best pulls most probably seen between WT Bosley and Sheen Farmers.

Alex Brown, from being in the team took over coaching from Sam Holland and later became a Grade 1 judge; in 1982 TOWA awarded him their highest honour, Award of Merit for long and distinguished service. The great success of the team was attributed to the members who were prepared to give total commitment to training, to the sport and to the club. They also won 10 European titles and 2 world titles.

Information supplied by Dorothy, Alex Brown's daughter.

Michael Eardley

We had a tug of war team at Rushton of local people; Bill Lockett was the coach. We competed at Bosley Sports and were runners up at 100 stone and they had a competition for teams that had never won a first prize to encourage teams to take part. The following year, George Oliver and Sam Holland asked me to join the Bosley Team. It was 1960 and I was 18.

We trained 2 or 3 nights a week for 2 hours and competed most weekends from May until September, generally on a Saturday but in later years on Sunday as well. Wood Treatment supplied a Bedford Dormobile for us to travel in.

It was a great experience for me to get my first 3As medal at White City; I'd never been that far before. For the 3As competitions we did 100 stone and Catchweight then in 1961 the TOW Association introduced 88 stone and later on there were also 96, 104, 108 and 113 and a Catchweight title. It got more serious for the younger and lighter men. Once a year for the TOW Association Championships all those competitions were held on one day; in 1980 at a Championship at Stanley Park, Blackpool I was in a 640kg competition with 96 teams.

Another very memorable trip was the 17 day invitation to South Africa in 1972. We pulled every other day - 5 tests and won every one. We came back with the highest honour any sportsman can bring out of Africa - a springbok's head! It was because we had won all the tests 2 pulls to nil.

At the World Championship out there again in 1976 the Sports Council paid a little for us to go as we were representing England, but it was very little compared to what athletes get today.

I dare say we couldn't have done it all without the support of Wood Treatment but I suppose our success was a great thing for them too. I did it for 20 years and have 160 medals and trophies because I was able to pull in several weights.

It was tremendous; I really enjoyed it and met a lot of grand folks. There were always 7 other good men and I enjoyed the social life with them. Five of us pulled together for 20 years: Norman Hyde, George Higton, Peter Hurst and Hilary Brown. You had to have a good relationship; we only fell out when they were on the other end of the rope in training!

TOW Association Championship 1960 catchweight winners.
Coach: Sam Holland
From back: Alec Brown, Hilary Brown, Geoff Bailey, Michael Eardley, Philip Boon,
Peter Hurst, George Higton, Norman Hyde

Back: Peter Hurst, Michael Eardley, Colin Brocklehurst, Hilary Brown
Front: Norman Hyde, Philip Boon, George Higton
Sam Holland giving orders

Main Road, Bosley

Extract from The Illustrated London News 4th August 1849

Nothing can exceed the natural beauty of the country almost the entire distance. On leaving North Rode, Cloud Hill is in full view and the line enters the valley of the Dane which it crosses by some lofty embankments. The same valley is intersected by the Macclesfield Canal as it winds its sinuous way amongst the hills on a series of embankments almost equally elevated and about a mile further still to the west, it is likewise crossed by the magnificent Dane Viaduct on the North Staffordshire main line. We question if three such gigantic and costly works as these two lines of railway and the canal are to be found in such close neighbourhood in any other part of the kingdom. The three can be seen at once by the traveller along either, or from the Leek and Macclesfield old mail road.

At Mill House Farm
Frank Whittaker left

Ernest Whittaker

James Massey

The Massey family arrived at Swallowdale Farm, Bosley about the year 1883. They had previously farmed at Walker Barn in the parish of Rainow. Swallowdale Farm consisted of 70 acres of reasonable pasture and meadow land and about the same amount of rough grazing and moorland, rising to a small grouse moor on Bosley Minn.

Great grandfather Joseph and his wife Martha and several children, including my grandfather Daniel came. In the early 1890s Daniel married Sarah Hadfield from Bell Farm, North Rode. They had 6 children, the third being my father William. He married my mother, Amy Etchells from Sutton in 1923 and took over the tenancy of Swallowdale, farming on his own account. My eldest sister, Margaret was born in 1924 and Barbara 5 years later. William and Amy had to wait 12 years for the greatest event of their life to happen - James William Massey was born!

Swallowdale 1920s

The German High Command got to hear of this and decided something must be done ASAP. A bomber was sent over to England to eliminate the problem and on a moonlit night the bomb was released but missed its target landing in a bottomless pit about 200 yards from the homestead where it remains to this day.

As I'm the last Massey to live at Swallowdale I would like to recall some field names. On the lower side of the farmyard there was Broad Meadow, Ringwood, Ringwood Meadow, Nursery Bank, Old Lane, Wheat Field, Marl Field and Old Meadow which was probably the last field in Bosley to be ploughed with a pair of horses. Then Big Field, Near Egg Croft, Middle Egg Croft, Far Egg Croft, Clough Pasture and Big Pasture.

Immediately in front of the house going up towards Bosley Minn was the Gore. On the top side of the farm buildings was the Nab, the Nab Wood, Near Ridding, Middle Ridding and Broad Knowl, while up on Bosley Minn were the Brown Hill and Black Hill.

It was a very sheltered farm at the head of two valleys and the first thing that you saw as you approached the farm up the drive was a big holly tree in front of the house which concealed the privy. They built a new privy down the garden path - a double one; one for the family and one for the workers.

Just after WW2 my cousin Dan Massey started to bring a troupe of Scouts from Gawsworth to camp on the hill. Soon after this, a much larger group of scouts from the Manchester area came during the Spring, Summer and Autumn, led by their scoutmaster, Stuart Gibbons.

Scouts visiting

As a little lad I was fascinated by all these scouts and longed to become one myself but as there was no scout group in Bosley, I never did. The main Scout Camp from Manchester was during Whit Week when between 30 and 40 Scouts would arrive. Initially all their equipment came on handcarts but latterly a bus was used.

The winters of 1947 and 1963 are the two worst winters in my memory. 1947 brought huge amounts of snow and together with the strong NE winds created enormous snow drifts everywhere. For almost two weeks dad had to hitch one of the horses to a sledge and take the milk churns cross-country over neighbours' land, wherever the wind had blown the snow away in order to meet the milk wagon on the main road. I can clearly remember one morning watching dad start off down the Clough Pasture with the load of milk churns when suddenly the sledge tipped over, the churn lids flew off and most, if not all of the milk joined the other white stuff on the ground - not a happy day!!

As there was no modern equipment to clear the snow, German POWs were drafted in to dig through the drifts. The great blizzard started at the end of January and it was well on into March before snow disappeared from the Bosley area and I am informed that it was late spring before the last snow disappeared from the hills between Macclesfield, Buxton and Leek.

James Massey and Roly Gilman

All photos at Swallowdale

James M, Arthur Gibson, Robert Nicklin

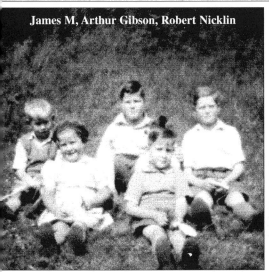

**1948 1st day out with
new tractor.
William Massey**

Possibly the last field in Bosley to be ploughed with a pair of horses

Barbara Massey on Jess

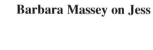

James and Hans

**Haymaking at
Swallowdale**

Roly

Barbara and James

**'Big Game Hunter!!' James
(double-barrelled cork gun)**

**Our abandoned
car in 1947**

Nurses Cottage, Main
Road, Bosley
Collection point for churns
1947

The German POWs who had worked to clear the snow after the 1947 blizzard came from a large POW camp at Toft near to Knutsford. When the war ended the authorities sent the POWs out daily to work on local farms. They were dropped off in the morning at the farm gates or at the bottom of the farm drive and had to walk the rest of the way to the farmstead. Dad applied to have one of these men and soon one would turn up each morning at about 9am. Sometimes we had the same man for several weeks or at other times we had 2 or 3 different men in a week.

There were various nationalities: Germans, Italians, Yugoslavs. One from Yugoslavia was obviously a born and bred farmer; he could work a pair of horses as well as anyone dad had ever had working for him. He was too good to be true and after 4 weeks some other farmer must have claimed him because we never saw him again!

After a time things settled into a regular routine and a German POW named Hans became our regular worker. He was a university graduate and found farm work very hard. His hands became very sore and blistered and to ease the pain he would cool them down in the brook which ran through the farmyard.

They were sent out each morning from camp with a couple of rounds of dry bread for their midday meal. Mother said you couldn't expect anyone to do a hard day's work on dry bread so she always gave them a good hot dinner like the rest of the family.

Christmas was coming and Hans thought that to show his gratitude he would make a traditional German child's toy for me. He had no money to buy anything so used whatever he could find to make this toy. So with little more than a sharpened dinner knife and a few bent nails and some odd bits of wood he created a masterpiece - a board with 4 hens on the top which when gently shaken, all the birds would peck the ground as if eating corn.

Swallowdale was a wonderful place for a young lad who was interested in wildlife to grow up in. Dad was always ready to draw my attention to signs of all the animals and birds that lived around. He knew where to find a partridge nest or baby rabbits' nest and if you were lucky, where to see woodpeckers searching in rotten trees for grubs. But the most interesting thing I ever saw I found myself. One day in summer I was wandering across the Brown Hill past a thorn tree when my attention was caught by a number of small birds and animals hanging impaled on the sharp thorns of the upper half of the tree; up to about a dozen in number. I didn't know what to make of this so I hurried home to study my bird reference books. After a short time I came across an account of a bird called a Common Shrike or to give it its country name, The Butcher Bird, and what I'd found was its larder. Apparently when food is plentiful, the Butcher Bird hangs surplus food from branches like I'd seen earlier in readiness for when food is scarce. I feel really privileged to have seen this because I haven't heard anyone refer to this spectacle since.

In my early days the only source of power at Swallowdale were the heavy horses. Shire horses were dad's favourite breed and I can just remember him having four. Before long one was disposed of because of old age; this left us with three: Jess, Titch and Fan. Jess was an independent soul who would work all day long if the spirit moved her but the next day could be just as awkward. The other two took each days work as it came and could work all day long whatever job they were put to. Heavy horses have often been described as gentle giants and so they were.

Tractors were slowly taking over from horses and so in the summer of 1948 dad joined the trend and bought a Standard Fordson tractor and trailer from Lichfield Machinery sale and so the reliance on horse power slowly came to an end. I don't think dad ever really took to tractors; his first love was the heavy horses.

One of the most amusing happenings I can remember being talked about was the time when one night in the middle of winter Dad took himself off for a pint or two at the Queens Arms in Bosley. Jack Gibson the water bailiff of Bosley Reservoir was in the tap room soon to be joined by Sam Booth the local poacher who lived in a shack on Bosley Cloud.

As it was a dark night with no moon and a strong wind blowing, it was an ideal time to go poaching rabbits with long nets. Sam Booth suggested the three of them should go after closing time at the pub and net Swythamley Park. 'There's always plenty of rabbits in Swythamley Park', he said, 'and best of all Sir Philip Brocklehurst, the owner is away in foreign parts on some expedition.'

After closing time they set off; Sam picked his bag of nets and pegs up from where hed left them in Bosley Churchyard before going into the Queens. Swythamley Park must be between 3 and 4 miles across country from the Queens Arms but even so our heroes made good time going by the Feeder path by Lower Minn End, through the big wood behind Higher Minn End, past Barley Ford Farm and over the River Dane by way of the rope bridge eventually arriving in Swythamley Park.

It would appear that somebody had been there before them; not one rabbit was seen or heard during the whole expedition.

Amy & Margaret Massey
with Grandad James Etchells

All they could do was to retrace their steps and put it down to experience; a round trip of getting on for 8 miles in pitch dark and nothing to show for it!

Muriel Johnson

We lived at Dawson Farm, Bosley; there were seven of us children. My dad, Eric Woodman Johnson milked about 40 cows. There were often tramps that would come and help a little on the farm; I think a lot of them were war casualties. One who helped us for several years was a Scotsman called Louie. He had his meals with us and was treated like one of the family but had a bed up in the loft. He worked on the farm and had a wage but never drew any money till come spring - mother saved the money - then he'd be gone for about two weeks until it was gone, usually on a drinking binge in Macclesfield. He showed us how to make tripods of hay like they do in Scotland. These were left in the field until you wanted them and then fetched with a horse and cart.

None of the farm was level; you needed one leg shorter than the other. It was quite wet clay farm and father used to do more work with the horse than the tractor because of getting the tractor stuck. We had a big work horse called Charlie who had been the last working horse on Manchester Railway hunting trucks.

At Dawson Farm

In the early 1950s there were some bad summers and hardly any dry fodder was got in, one particularly so bad in wintertime they went with the horse and cart and Louie scythed the grass in the meadows and they dragged it back to feed the cows. It was nearly all they had that winter, only fill-belly, but they got through.

Mrs Johnson

Mother went off shopping one day and Louie was drunk so she locked him in the house and left him looking after us children and I can remember being sat on his knee and he was giving me whisky. He was usually sober and kind and we loved him.

Looking back I remember all the farmers sent some milk and that they used the term surrey or sirree when addressing their mates.

**At Dawson
Farm**

Mr Johnson

Evelyn Naden

I was born and brought up at Goldenhill Farm in the parish of Bosley on the border of Sutton and Wincle. There is a cornerstone where the three parishes join. I remember the bad winter of 1947. My father Ernest, my brother Alfred and Sam Bullock from Dollards dug out 3 times and it kept filling it back in; Wincle was cut off for 12 days.

In 1940 my father had the first tractor in the area, a Fordson and he worked for the War Ag doing ploughing and he had a self binder and did contract work along with Mr Shuker who had a little thrashing box. Then father had one from the War Ag which he later bought and they did threshing all around the area from Rainow through to Gawsworth

Feb 1947

Dollards Farm Drive

and North Rode. He was very busy and left me and my mother doing the milking and farm work. We milked 24 cows by hand then had one of the first milking machines. Father was quite progressive; we didn't have electricity but he rigged something up from the engine when we milked that charged wet batteries and made electricity - 50 volts for lights and we could iron with a plug into a light socket when they were milking.

Some Manchester businessmen had a shoot based at Goldenhill. They started on the 12th August, the opening of the grouse shooting season and came every fortnight on a Wednesday until February. They used to do one drive on Sutton Common and the next on Bosley Minns alternately. In 1938 it was quite a big affair and they had Agars from Manchester in to do the catering. Mother reared ducks and they cooked ten for lunch. Some of the ducks were reared for shooting but they were very wise after the first shoot and flew too high for the guns.

It was mostly grouse; there was a lot of heather then. Father always knew where there was a bunch of white heather and used to bring a sprig back for mother but he never told us where he found it. As a child I used to earn money for beating, usually a shilling though one man was very generous and gave us half a crown. The beagles from

Sutton used to come 2 or 3 times during the season too.

I remember hearing corncrakes and seeing snipe and a lot of peewits. In wartime the air force radar post on Sutton Common used to raid the nests for eggs. There were also lots of skylarks.

In 1944 an American plane crashed at Dawson Farm on Swans Lake Field. Mr Naden and his 13 year old son Maurice ran to the burning aircraft while his other son ran to a neighbouring farm to phone for help. They managed to rescue two men but one later died from his injuries. They were each awarded a Kings Commendation for Conduct signed on behalf of the King by Winston Churchill.

Goldenhill 1940s

Mary and Ernest Bullock

In this photo of a shooting party at Swallowdale in the late 1930s, my father is on the right. In the centre is myself, Betty Hill and Barbara Massey. Behind us is Stanley Hill who was the boss of UCP, United Cattle Products. They were tripe dressers and had big premises in Manchester and a restaurant in Macclesfield.
Next left is Mr Lavender, Uncle William Massey, Mr Rogers who was in textiles and Mr Clifford Frost the owner of a dairy at Didsbury who took our milk. On the left again is JB Rennie who in wartime used to send us bomb damaged parcels of material which I made dresses from.

The War finished the shooting parties.

**Threshing at Ball Greave,
Macclesfield Forest**

**Haymaking at
Goldenhill pre-war**

**Maurice Naden with
his sister Mabel at
Dawson Farm mid-
1930s**

Mid 1930s at Goldenhill

Donald Wheelton 1930

**Frank and Annie Whittaker, Abraham and
Blanch Bullock, at Sourbutts Bosley**

**Uncle Walter
Wheelton**

**Uncle Dan at Swallowdale
1930s**

Alfred Bullock. Winter Stories

In 1941 my father had to take the milk to the cross roads with the horse and sledge. It was an ex-army horse and when they got to the reservoir they met the Welsh Fusiliers marching along with spades on their shoulders on their way to dig through the snow drifts. He said that the horse pricked up its ears and clearly remembered them after over 20 years. The snow drifts were so deep that at Golden Slack Farm next door they had to dig a tunnel to get out of the house and there were rabbit tracks on the house roof.

In 1947 the water pipes were all frozen up so we had to let the cattle to the troughs in the yard. The snow was so deep and hard that they walked over the five-bar gate into the field. On May Fair day Mr Bowler who farmed at Clough House Farm at Wildboarclough took bets in the Nags Head at Macclesfield that he could bring a bucketful of snow. He won his bet.

In 1998 I had my moment of glory. I was taking a bale of hay to my sheep when a policeman stopped me and asked if I would give an interview for Sky TV. Two ladies with long boots and fur hats took a photo of me digging a sheep from a drift near a wall. That night on Sky News I appeared for 30 seconds with the title, Farmer rescues sheep on Cheshire Hills.

Goldenhill 1941

Sam and Alfred middle and right

Wincle